MAKING MALCOLM

KT-118-064

MAKING MALCOLM

The Myth and Meaning of Malcolm X

MICHAEL ERIC DYSON

UNIVERSITY OF WOLVERHAMPTON
LIBRARY

Acc No. 2099897

CONTROL
019509235X

DATE 26 FEB. 1997

SITE DY

CLASS

323·
1196
073
DYS

OXFORD UNIVERSITY PRESS
New York   Oxford

Oxford University Press

Oxford   New York
Athens   Auckland   Bangkok   Bombay
Calcutta   Cape Town   Dar es Salaam   Delhi
Florence   Hong Kong   Istanbul   Karachi
Kuala Lumpur   Madras   Madrid   Melbourne
Mexico City   Nairobi   Paris   Singapore
Taipei   Tokyo   Toronto

and associated companies in
Berlin   Ibadan

Copyright © 1995 by Michael Eric Dyson

First published in 1995 by Oxford University Press, Inc.,
198 Madison Avenue, New York, New York 10016

First issued as an Oxford University Press paperback, 1996

Oxford is a registered trademark of Oxford University Press

All rights reserved. No part of this publication may be reproduced,
stored in a retrieval system, or transmitted, in any form or by any means,
electronic, mechanical, photocopying, recording, or otherwise,
without the prior permission of Oxford University Press.

Library of Congress Cataloging-in-Publication Data
Dyson, Michael Eric.
Making Malcolm : the myth and meaning of Malcolm X /
Michael Eric Dyson.
p.   cm.
ISBN 0-19-509235-X
ISBN 0-19-510285-1 (Pbk.)
1. X, Malcolm, 1925–1965.   I. Title.
BP223.Z8L573338   1994   320.5'4'092—dc20   94-16396

X by Amiri Baraka, Copyright © by Amiri Baraka. Reprinted by permission
of Sterling Lord Literistic, Inc.

"What I'm Telling You" by Elizabeth Alexander, Copyright © by Elizabeth
Alexander. Reprinted by permission of the author.

10 9 8 7 6 5 4 3 2 1

Printed in the United States of America

For my marvelous son Michael Eric Dyson, II,
who, like Malcolm, is tall and intelligent
and who keeps the spirit of Malcolm alive
in his willingness to question

PREFACE
TEACHING MALCOLM

We don't judge a man because of the color of his skin. We don't judge you because you're white; we don't judge you because you're black; we don't judge you because you're brown. We judge you because of what you do and what you practice.

Malcolm X, in *Malcolm X: The Last Speeches*

"Professor Dyson, what you did was wrong, man," my student bellowed at me across my desk, supported by three of his equally angry classmates.

"You embarrassed us in front of all those people."

"No! What y'all did was wrong," I fired back at him. "You embarrassed and dissed me in front of the whole class."

I had just stormed out of the classroom and up the stairs to my space in the bank of second-floor offices in Churchill House, the building that houses Afro-American Studies at Brown, with my four accusers chasing closely behind. A full hour and a half before my seminar on Malcolm X was due to end for the day, I had publicly scolded these students— all young, black, male, and very bright—for what I felt was intolerable behavior.

"I will not put up with this any more," I angrily announced as I interrupted the class on the heels of a remark from one of the young men that proved to be the final straw.

"You have held this class hostage to your narrow beliefs and rude behavior from the very beginning. And since you've made a big deal of being a black male in this class, I resent how you've treated me—a black man—with great disrespect in my own course. Class is over."

This had never happened to me before in all my teaching career, not at Hartford Seminary, not at Chicago Theological Seminary, and not at Brown, though I had faced tough situations in each place. I felt a mixture of embarrassment and anger because I'd lost control of the class and myself, something I hadn't done even when I endured bruising battles as a pastor of three Baptist churches in the South. But I felt I had no choice.

The conflict had been building to an inevitable climax the entire semester. I knew that a seminar on a figure as explosively controversial as Malcolm X would mimic disagreements about him in other quarters of American culture. Like fiercely contested discussions about Malcolm in the popular press and in scholarly books, a seminar on Malcolm would provoke heated exchanges between students as they debated his intellectual meaning and cultural significance for black people, and for a nation that misunderstood and often reviled him when he was alive.

This proved to be true when I taught the seminar at

Brown during the previous semester. My students engaged in intense scrutiny of Malcolm's writings and pored over the secondary literature that addressed his thought and career. There were representatives from across the ideological, political, and racial spectrum in that seminar of twenty students. There were Asians and Latinas, conservatives and radicals, blacks and whites, men and women. There were black neonationalists as well as more moderate integrationists. There were students who deployed densely laden theoretical perspectives popular in post structuralism seated next to students whose unfamiliarity with the intricacies of race and class marked their beginner's pace. But the class worked because all of us fought, sometimes with ferocious abandon, sometimes with subtle restraint, over Malcolm's meaning in an environment that encouraged intellectual rigor and respect for the cantankerous differences that abounded.

Ironically, the success of my first Malcolm X seminar at Brown made me vulnerable to the sorts of problems that plagued its second incarnation a mere semester later. From the first day of class, it became obvious that this seminar possessed a dynamic that razed any arguments about race not rooted in personal experience or black cultural authority. Each class became a highly ritualized installment in a morality play about the tension between good and evil. In the case of my seminar, this conflict was crudely reduced to the tension between black and white, and, in other instances, between bourgeois and ghetto (read "authentically black") cultural and political expressions.

This narrowly conceived and troubling vision of authentic racial discourse reflects the character of debates about race now taking place in a country reeling from the implications of multiculturalism, ethnic and sexual difference, and identity politics. Often the proponents of narrow notions of racial, ethnic, or sexual identity are simply responding to the egregious and increasingly unremarked-on offenses heaped on them in a culture that remains, in crucial ways, uncomfortable with their heightened visibility. To make matters worse, blacks, gays and lesbians, Latinos and Latinas, feminists, the ghetto poor, and other minorities who defend themselves in public are often attacked under the banner of crusades against "political correctness."

"P.C." has become the common rallying cry of conservatives, liberals, and radicals, many of whom harbor resentments against the assertive presence and practices of formerly excluded minorities who no longer need representation by proxy. When these minorities show up to speak for themselves, and often in terms that are radically different from how stereotyping or scapegoating has made them appear, there is resistance from friend and foe alike. The plausible complaints that can be launched against debilitating conceptions of racial, sexual, or political identity (after all, the term "political correctness" was invented by the left to get its own house in order) are lost as anti–p.c. forces lose a sense of proportion. By and large, racial, sexual, and political minorities don't control resources or wield power in ways comparable to those used by the people and powers they oppose.

This doesn't mean that the legitimate battles that some minorities fight are not occasionally fraught with self-defeating tactics of defense that trump their highest aims. This was quite evident in my Malcolm X seminar during that second semester. It showed innocuously in small matters like the patterns of white and black bodies grouped by race in the classroom. But it was revealed more menacingly in the rigid racial reasoning of several black males who appealed to Malcolm's masculinity, his blackness, and his ghetto grounding as the basis for their strict identification with him. In their eyes, such a strategy lent their interpretations of the leader a natural advantage.

The unyielding insistence of my black male students that a racial litmus test be evoked through highly charged personal narrative (the sort of jockeying for privilege of the "because I'm black, poor, male and angry I understand him better than you" variety that I wanted to avoid) made class time a wearying exercise in either defending or defeating racial borders. The examination of ideological justifications for racist practices, or an in-depth investigation of the links between racial and class oppression—in short, the kinds of analysis that undoubtedly would have contributed to their

cause—was constantly put off by appeals to a severely lim-
iting politics of experience and authenticity.

Now I am not one of those black intellectuals who argues for a strategic point of Archimedean objectivity beyond
the realm of slashing ideological conflict, longing wistfully
for a neutral zone free of the fracturing results of racial politics. Neither am I committed to the belief that if Americans
simply understood more about one another we could do
better or that through knowledge alone, we could achieve
a racial nirvana signalled in Rodney King's desperate plea
that "we all get along." I understand that so much of our
nation's claims of racial peace are haunted by the hypocrisy
of hidden white power and concealed bigotry. I know that
a great deal of discourse about race is trapped in abstraction
and avoidance as we ingeniously seek to deflect the link
between past injustices and present injuries.

But I also know that the game of proving you're blacker
than the next Negro, an art engaged in and encouraged by
Malcolm at various stages of his career, can have disastrous
results. Not only does it set in motion a rancid Aristotelian
regression back to a mythic "real blackness" that spins on
endlessly, but it borrows from a peculiarly European quest
for racial purity, a troubling Manichaean mind-set that dis-
tinguishes between "us" and "them." This is precisely the
sort of thinking that anyone paying careful attention to the
complex workings of black culture in Africa and throughout
the diaspora cannot help but abhor.

Moreover, Malcolm's cultural renaissance—his improbable second coming—brims with irony. Our era is marked by vigorous debates about racial authenticity and selling-out, and about the consequences of crossing over to larger markets to increase mass appeal. Participants in these debates, which include not only my seminar, but everyone from politicians to rap artists, often draw on Malcolm's scorching rebukes to such moves. Meanwhile, Malcolm's X is marketed in countless business endeavors and is stylishly branded on baseball hats and T-shirts by every age, race, and gender. So much for the politics of purity.

But no matter how powerfully or with how many different examples I plied many of my black male students, they remained suspicious of any attempt to divorce Malcolm from his exclusive meaning for young, black, angry males. In many ways, they were fighting over Malcolm's tall body and short life, allowing no dibs on a legacy they felt Malcolm had bequeathed to them alone. They seemed to be saying, "White folk have ripped off so much of black culture; they can't have Malcolm too." Their black neonationalist politics led them to lay claim to Malcolm's mantle, and Malcolm's moral authority supplied support for their gestures of reappropriating his image.

Malcolm's moral authority was fueled by a moral magnetism so great that it continues to attract people who were not yet born when he met his gruesome death. Malcolm possessed an unperturbable quality that my students found irresistible: he fixed his sight on the racial goals to be obtained and pursued them with unvarying zeal. This single-mindedness is especially true of the period when, under the spell of Nation of Islam leader Elijah Muhammad's scheme of evil by colors, he pummeled the notion of black cultural inferiority with consummate skill. He eventually grew suspicious of the conclusions about race that insular versions of nationalism entail. He also gained distance on the indiscriminate demonizing of color that had already imposed severe penalties on black people's lives. He achieved a moral maturity that gave him a more complex view of the possibilities of human community across the racial divide.

Admittedly, it is difficult to highlight Malcolm's moral maturity in the midst of the contemporary reemergence of racism, a fact that many of my black male students were right to point out. In large part, Malcolm's renewed presence on the cultural scene has been made possible by students like them and by others who've kept the flame of Malcolm's life burning brightly in black nationalist book stores and community gatherings across the nation while Malcolm was out of vogue. Such groups have held up Malcolm's Promethean accomplishments of mind and body—which constitute a style of black leadership barely glimpsed in our age—as models of black cultural achievement.

More than that, Malcolm's moral authority remains intact because he wasn't given to the kind of racial hustling that often passes for leadership. No, he wasn't against using the hustling tactics he gleaned from his years on the street to portray the crimes of white racism. He knew how to rhetorically master black and white opponents. But he rarely allowed that hustling ethic to distort his relations to the black people he selflessly loved. He rarely lost sight of the fact that he was the servant, not the master, of their best hopes and bravest dreams. Malcolm's love of black people made my black male students love him in return.

But they weren't willing to subject Malcolm, the object of their devotion, to rigorous criticism. Uncritical devotion cuts across Malcolm's mature skepticism about blindly following leaders. Malcolm learned that bitter lesson in the deadly fallout of his dissociation from Elijah Muhammad, whom he had once passionately adored. Malcolm wasn't perfect, and he knew it. And those of us who want to capture some of Malcolm's magic—and to learn through critical analysis of his failures and successes, his weaknesses and strengths—don't have to make him an idol.

Malcolm's moral authority finally consisted in telling the truth about our nation as best he could. He damned its moral hypocrisy and insincerity in trying to aid the people it had harmed for so long, a fact that created seething pockets of rage within the corporate black psyche. Malcolm blessed our rage by releasing it. His tall body was a vessel for our outrage at the way things were and always had been for most black people, especially those punished by poverty and forced to live in enclaves of urban terror. It was their desire to reclaim Malcolm for themselves and to display their superior grasp of black culture that motivated many of my black male students to take my Malcolm X seminar, as I was to later discover in our confrontation in my office.

"We get tired of going to classes and having white students discuss things they don't know about, while we take a back seat and remain quiet," one of my students told me.

"When we came in the first day and saw how many white students were signed up for this class, we had a decision to make," another related to me. "We could either do like we usually do, and just say 'forget it,' because they weren't going to understand us anyway, or *we* could take charge and be the ones to set the pace."

Although I could figure out why they didn't want to let the white students have Malcolm, I found it off-putting and a bit bizarre, maybe even disingenuous, that their efforts excluded me too. After all, if the best chance of understanding Malcolm, as they often reminded me, depended on the possibility of having as close to an experience of life as Malcolm had had, then I certainly qualified, perhaps even more than they did.

I was born in 1958 in Detroit's inner city, my age, ghetto experience, and geographic proximity to his childhood digs giving me a link to Malcolm's life not immediately suggested by my students' experiences. Like Malcolm, I was reared in a large clan. My immediate family included my parents and four brothers, plus four older step-siblings who lived on their own. My father was a factory laborer; my mother, a para-professional with the Detroit public schools. Neither had been to college. My father was laid off from his job as master set-up man at Kelsey Hayes Wheel-brake and Drum Company after thirty-three years of faithful service.

After that, he started Dyson and Sons grass-cutting and sodding business, with three of us boys working with him. That work, plus our work at Morton's Nursery every day after I got home from school in the seventh grade, and later at Sam's Drugstore—besides foraging the city's alleys in search of discarded steel and iron we could turn in at the junk yard for a modest sum of money—kept us from fully going on welfare. (We did receive food stamps at one time.) Money was tight, and times were tough.

Although I received a scholarship to Cranbrook, a prestigious secondary school thirty miles from Detroit in the rich suburb of Bloomfield Hills, I left after two years and received a diploma from "night school" at Northwestern High School. Shortly after graduation at eighteen, I got my twenty-six-year-old girlfriend pregnant, and married her before our son was born in 1978. I worked at a variety of jobs (and at one time, two full-time jobs simultaneously), from fast-food to maintenance jobs, from construction work to hustling painting gigs, before I was fired from a job at Chrysler one month before my son was born. My wife and I had no insurance to cover his birth. Welfare was our only option. And as with many shotgun marriages plagued by poverty, ours misfired. We divorced scarcely a year after we'd been married.

I didn't go south to attend college until I was twenty-one. By then, I had become a Baptist minister, and I pastored three churches, and worked in a factory in Knoxville, Tennessee, to put myself through school. I graduated magna cum laude from Carson-Newman College (the first person in my family to graduate from college) and then received an M.A. and a Ph.D. in religion from Princeton University. By the time I sat before my students at Brown, I not only had been held up twice at gunpoint, but also had been a veteran of countless battles against racial, gender, and class oppression. Also I'd been virtually the sole financial supporter of my younger brother Everett's attempt to free himself from a life sentence in prison for second-degree murder. I was no stranger to young, black, angry males. I had been one, and depending on who's consulted, I'm still considered in the running. And yet, as I was to learn in our heated conflict in my office, these black males were suspicious of me from the very beginning.

"We wondered why you were teaching this course," one of the young men said, relaying a conversation they'd had earlier. "We wanted to know what your motive was for teaching a course on Malcolm." Having been a poor, angry black male who was also a preacher and from the same state where Malcolm spent his childhood wasn't enough, I guess. But I also knew that many of the young black males who were suspicious of me were greatly exaggerating their homeboy-from-the-hood backgrounds; most of them were well-to-do kids from upper-middle-class homes.

Their suspicions obviously extended to other members of the class. Time and again, in ways that were sometimes subtle, sometimes painfully conspicuous, the black males drew boundaries around Malcolm that kept even black females at bay. Sure, in the scheme of things black women had a greater chance of understanding Malcolm than, say, white men and women, but their gender prevented their complete comprehension. The hierarchy of interpretation the black males established, at once laughable and lamentable, only provoked further feelings of injury in the rest of the class.

Throughout the semester, several class members—black and white women and men, Asian and mixed-race students—came to me to vent their frustrations about many of my black male students. I felt awkward in hearing their complaints, and mostly agreeing with them. I understood what my black male students were up to, even though we were at cross-purposes as to what to make of the seminar's weekly three hours. I even gently chided the white students who came to me in private to express their bewilderment.

"I understand your feelings, even empathize with them," I told a white female student. "But we can't have a class on Malcolm X and not expect to feel some of the heat and passion he generated. The anger of some of these young black men mirrors the anger of Malcolm X.''

''You're right, Professor Dyson,'' she responded. ''I agree with you. But some of these men think it's all right to sleep with white women—'cuz some of them have slept with white women *in* our seminar. But when we make statements in class, even statements that might support Malcolm X, they frown at us.''

I was sorely tempted to divulge this bit of information in the next seminar, all in the interest, mind you, of making the greatest amount of data available as we debated the precise role of experience in racial politics. But alas, cooler instincts prevailed. (My student's story reminded me of a humorous exchange between Jesse Jackson and some militant black nationalists who were criticizing him as a sellout. As he pointed out that they all had white girlfriends, they informed Jackson, ''We're punishing their fathers.'')

I detected, too, in the classroom exchanges between me and the black males who trailed me to my office, a generational rift whose accusing distance I had, I believed until then, successfully overcome.

''We're talking about Onyx, about 'Baccdafuccup,' '' one of the black men said the first day of class, referring to a rap group and its album that had garnered critical praise for its street-savvy lyrics and its barely tempered rage. ''That's who expresses what we're talking about.''

Of course, there were more gentle signs of a perception

that I was no longer "young," such as the time I recently testified before a U.S. Senate subcommittee hearing on gangsta' rap. I quoted verbatim, from memory, the lyrics to a song by rapper Snoop Doggy Dogg while making a complex defense of gangsta' rappers, even as I scored their misogyny and homophobia.

"My, man," beamed a young black male in the audience who sought me out after the hearings that day, his hand extended to me in a gesture of brotherly affirmation.

"For a guy your age, you really can flow."

His compliment reminded me that while my thirty-five years made me a young man in the academy, it granted me outsider "adult" status with many young blacks.

But I also knew that more than generational forces were at work, more than age separated me from my younger compatriots. In fact, I believed that, based on his moral perspective, Malcolm X most likely would have disdained rap's materialistic impulses to get paid, spurned its hedonistic joie de vivre, its celebration of vulgar verbal expression. Hip-hop's sexual and rhetorical liberation might well have been Malcolm's moral chaos. But such dissonances between Malcolm and my young black male students went largely unnoticed, even as a basis for criticizing Malcolm's black moral puritanism, a force that surely challenged their way of life.

Malcolm's further contradictions, and the conflicting uses to which his legacy can be put, came home to me as I traveled during Thanksgiving recess to lecture on Malcolm in the Netherlands. After my public presentation, I was engaged in debate by a renowned Dutch writer, Stephan Sanders, who is black, is openly gay, and was reared in a white Dutch Jewish family. Sanders insisted that Malcolm was "far more American than he wanted to acknowledge," a product of an American culture that was obsessed with racial purity.

Sanders contended that Malcolm's lifelong struggle against domination showed classic signs of the "colonial dilemma." "The real dilemma is that being a black American as Malcolm called himself, [means that] he was born an American. So America is a . . . part of him." For Sanders, the "question is how one can definitely free oneself from the colonizer [while recognizing] that the colonizer is within you." His observations about Malcolm's internal struggles for a liberated consciousness were poignant, even moving.

Sanders couldn't understand why I voiced critical support for Malcolm, since it seemed that, as an opponent of racial essentialism, homophobia, and ethnic bigotry, I was in direct conflict with Malcolm's values. I responded that Malcolm was a complex figure, that his thought evolved, and that his moral vision was transformed over the course of a complicated, heroic life. Without either romanticizing Malcolm or making his memory a mere metaphor of rage, and thereby softening his palpable threat to black and white

defenders of the status quo, I attempted to argue Malcolm's use in a progressive politics that was racially *conscious*, but not racially *exclusive*. The mature Malcolm, I contended, was open to a range of political negotiations of identity and ideology that promoted lasting liberation. That Malcolm, I claimed, was a figure who could be celebrated and put to use internationally by despised and degraded people, even as his radical edge was being rounded off by worldwide commercialization.

I felt a deep gratification in communicating the meaning of Malcolm X to an international audience in a way that I had been prevented from doing closer to home. Maybe it was that sense of foreign appreciation that helped emphasize, perhaps even exaggerate, the struggles for clarity of Malcolm's meaning I experienced back at Brown. It was not long after my return home that my class exploded and that most of my students came to me that night, heaving a collective sigh of relief, saying that they'd wished that I had dramatically confronted many of my black male students earlier.

I couldn't derive much consolation from their sentiments, as much as I personally benefitted from hearing them. I knew that many of the fears that my black males harbored—that Malcolm would be done in by sell-out Negroes, that his sometimes harsh words would be soft-pedaled to suit the crossover ambitions of people pimping off of Malcolm's newfound popularity—had already been ominously realized. In my office after the seminar's abrupt dismissal, I warned my black male students that too often conclusions about who is deemed "in" or "out" of black cultural style are based on flimsy evidence, on slippery surfaces of judgment that don't account for complexity of belief or depth of commitment.

But I also assured them that my opposition to their tendentious arguments and uselessly divisive techniques in class grew out of a deep love for them. With tears streaming down my cheeks, I confessed that I pushed them hard, yes, perhaps harder than my white students, because I expected more from them. If they were to be fearless warriors in the battle against racial oppression, then they must be prepared to wage fierce *intellectual* combat that was rooted in persuasive argumentation as well as edifying passion.

"We didn't realize that you felt this way," one of them offered as consolation to my obvious distress. "We didn't know that when you did what you did in class that you cared for us."

"Of course I care for you," I said. "You're my brothers. You're precious to me. You're precious to our race. You all have brilliant futures."

"Well, if we did anything to embarrass you, we're sorry," another replied. "We were only trying to defend ourselves."

"And if I did anything to hurt or embarrass you, I'm truly sorry," I offered in return. After this, I embraced each one of them, and we parted with the mutual benediction to "stay strong."

I am not suggesting by this seemingly sappy ending that my black male students and I don't have profound disagreements about Malcolm's meaning for our people or nation. We do. Neither do I mean that a late-evening embrace and show of solidarity between me and my black male students wiped away the hurt feelings that either side may have endured in the skirmishes that occurred over much of the seminar. It probably didn't.

What that encounter did accomplish, however, is a renewed determination on my part to make Malcolm available to the wider audience that he deserves without making him a puppet for moderate, mainstream purposes, and without freighting him with the early bigotries and blindnesses he grew to discard. Ironically, my black male students' abrasive resistance helped me understand the urgency of such a task. All of us who have a stake in the meaning and myth of Malcolm's life will continue to do battle, will continue to disagree about how and why Malcolm's memory is used in one way or another, even as we make wildly different uses of his career. From filmmakers to intellectuals, from hip-hop artists to community organizers, we are together involved in the process of exploring and

Preface

evaluating the making of Malcolm's legacy. This book is a contribution to that enterprise.

Providence   M.E.D.
May 19, 1994 (Malcolm's birthday)

ACKNOWLEDGMENTS

I would like to thank my wonderful editor, Liz Maguire, for bringing this book to Oxford and for making its production such sheer pleasure. Her support of the book and its author is largely responsible for its appearance. I would also like to thank Elda Rotor and the other folk at Oxford who assisted with the book for their tireless energy in assisting Liz and me on this project. I would also like to thank my wonderful children, Michael, Mwata, and Maisha, for their love and support. I am grateful to my mother, Addie Mae Dyson, for her continued love and devotion, and to my brothers Anthony, Gregory, and Brian for their interest in my work. For my brother Everett, prisoner 212687, I am grateful for his intelligent conversation and his will to be free; stay strong and keep the faith! I am grateful to my thoughtful niece and nephew, Mejai and Torkwase Dyson, for their stimulating conversation. I am also thankful for the extremely helpful critical comments of William Van Deburg and Robin D. G. Kelley. And for my precious friend D. Soyini Madison, I am grateful for intellectual and spiritual companionship. And, of course, for my intelligent, beautiful wife, Marcia, I reserve

Acknowledgments

special gratitude for her inexhaustible store of loyalty and love, and for her belief in me and this book.

Portions of this manuscript have appeared in much different form than published here in *Social Text, Tikkun,* and *Christian Century.*

CONTENTS

MAKING MALCOLM

1
MEETING MALCOLM

First, I don't profess to be anybody's leader. I'm one of
22 million Afro-Americans, all of whom have suffered
the same things. And I probably cry out a little louder
against the suffering than most others and therefore,
perhaps, I'm better known. I don't profess to have a
political, economic, or social solution to a problem as
complicated as the one which our people face in the
States, but I am one of those who is willing to try *any
means necessary* to bring an end to the injustices that
our people suffer.

Malcolm X, in *By Any Means Necessary: Speeches,
Interviews, and a Letter, by Malcolm X*

Malcolm X, one of the most complex and enigmatic African-
American leaders ever, was born Malcolm Little on May 19,
1925, in Omaha, Nebraska. Since his death in 1965, Malcolm's life has increasingly acquired mythic stature. Along
with Martin Luther King, Jr., Malcolm is a member of the
pantheon of twentieth-century black saints. Unlike that of
King, however, Malcolm's heroic rise was both aided and
complicated by his championing of black nationalism and
his advocacy of black self-defense against white racist violence.

Malcolm's ideas of black nationalism were shaped virtually from the womb by the example of his parents, Earl

and Louise Little, both members of Marcus Garvey's Universal Negro Improvement Association (UNIA). As president of the Omaha branch of the UNIA, Earl Little, who was also an itinerant Baptist preacher, vigorously proclaimed the Garveyite doctrine of racial self-help and black unity, often with Malcolm at his side. Louise Little served as reporter of the Omaha UNIA. A native of Grenada, Louise was a deeply spiritual woman who presided over her brood of eight children even as she endured the abuse of her husband, and together they heaped domestic violence on their children.

According to Malcolm, his family was driven from Omaha by the Ku Klux Klan while he was still an infant, forcing them to seek safer habitation in Lansing, the capital city of Michigan eighty miles northwest of Detroit. Their respite was only temporary, however; the Little family house was burned down by a white hate group, the Black Legionnaires, during Malcolm's early childhood in 1929. This experience of racial violence, which Malcolm termed his "earliest vivid memory," deeply influenced his unsparing denunciation of white racism during his public career as a black nationalist leader.

When Malcolm was only six, his father died after being crushed under a streetcar. It is unclear whether Earl died at the hands of the Black Legionnaires, as Malcolm reports in his autobiography, or whether his death was accidental, as recent scholarship has suggested.[1] In either case, his loss

4

bore fateful consequences for the Little family because Lou-ise Little was faced with raising eight children alone during the Great Depression. She eventually suffered a mental breakdown, and her children were dispersed to different foster homes.

Malcolm's life after his family's breakup went from bleak to desperate, as he was shuttled between several fos-ter homes. Malcolm stole food to survive and began devel-oping hustling habits that he later perfected in Boston, where he went to live with his half-sister Ella after dropping out of school in Lansing after completing the eighth grade. Before leaving school, Malcolm had become eighth-grade class president at Mason Junior High School. But a devas-tating rebuff from a teacher—who discouraged Malcolm in his desire to become an attorney by claiming that it was an unrealistic goal for "niggers"—finally sealed Malcolm's early fate as an academic failure.

It was in Boston that Malcolm encountered for the first time the black bourgeoisie, with its social pretensions and exaggerated rituals of cultural self-affirmation, leading him to conclude later that the black middle class was largely in-effective in achieving authentic black liberation. It was also in Boston's Roxbury and New York's Harlem that Malcolm was introduced to the street life of the northern urban poor and working class, gaining crucial insight about the cultural styles, social sufferings, and personal aspirations of every-day black people. Malcolm's hustling repertoire ranged from drug dealing and numbers running to burglary, the last activity landing him in a penitentiary for a six- to ten-year sentence. Malcolm's prison period—lasting from 1946 to 1952—marked the first of several extraordinary transformations he underwent as he searched for the truth about himself and his relation to black consciousness, black freedom and unity, and black religion.

While in prison, Malcolm read widely and argued passionately about a broad scope of subjects, from biblical theology to Western philosophy, voraciously absorbing the work of authors as diverse as Louis S. B. Leakey and Friedrich Nietzsche. Malcolm read so much during this period that his eyesight became strained, and he began wearing his trademark glasses. It was during his prison stay that Malcolm experienced his first religious conversion, slowly evolving from a slick street hustler and con artist to a sophisticated, self-taught devotee of Elijah Muhammad and the Nation of Islam, the black nationalist religious group that Muhammad headed. Malcolm was drawn to the Nation of Islam because of the character of its black nationalist practices and beliefs: its peculiar gift for rehabilitating black male prisoners; its strong emphasis on black pride, history, culture, and unity; and its unblinking assertion that white men were devils, a belief that led Muhammad and his followers to advocate black separation from white society.

Within a year of his release from prison on parole in 1952, Malcolm became a minister with the Nation of Islam, journeying to its Chicago headquarters to meet face to face with the man whose theological doctrines of white evil and black racial superiority had given Malcolm new life. Through a herculean work ethic and spartan self-discipline—key features of the black puritanism that characterized the Nation's moral orientation—Malcolm worked his way in short order from assistant minister of Detroit's Temple Number One to national spokesman for Elijah Muhammad and the Nation of Islam. In his role as the mouthpiece for the Nation of Islam, Malcolm brought unprecedented visibility to a religious group that many critics had either ignored or dismissed as fundamentalist fringe fanatics. Under Malcolm's leadership, the Nation grew from several hundred to a hundred thousand members by the early 1960s. The Nation under Malcolm also produced forty temples throughout the United States and purchased thirty radio stations.

During the late 1950s and early 1960s, enormous changes were rapidly occurring within American society in regard to race. The momentous *Brown* v. *Board of Education* Supreme Court decision, delivered in 1954, struck down the "separate-but-equal" law that had enforced racially segregated public education since 1896. And in 1955, the historic bus boycott in Montgomery, Alabama—sparked by seamstress Rosa Parks's refusal to surrender her seat to a white passenger, as legally mandated by a segregated public-transportation system—brought its leader, Martin Luther King, Jr., to national prominence. King's fusion of black

MEETING MALCOLM

Christian civic piety and traditions of American public morality and radical democracy unleashed an irresistible force
on American politics that fundamentally altered the social
conditions of millions of blacks, especially the black middle
classes in the South.

The civil rights movement, though, barely affected the
circumstances of poor southern rural blacks. Neither did it
greatly enhance the plight of poor northern urban blacks,
whose economic status and social standing were severely
handicapped by forces of deindustrialization: the rise of au-
tomated technology that displaced human wage earners,
the severe decline in manufacturing and in retail and
wholesale trade, and escalating patterns of black unemployment. These social and economic trends, coupled with
the growing spiritual despair that beginning in the early
1950s gripped Rust Belt cities like New York, Chicago, Philadelphia, Detroit, Cleveland, Indianapolis, and Baltimore,
did not initially occupy the social agenda of the southern-
based civil rights movement.

Malcolm's ministry, however, as was true of the Nation
of Islam in general, was directed toward the socially dispossessed, the morally compromised, and the economically
desperate members of the black proletariat and ghetto poor
who were unaided by the civil rights movement. The Nation
of Islam recruited many of its members among the prison
populations largely forgotten by traditional Christianity
(black and white). The Nation also proselytized among the

hustlers, drug dealers, pimps, prostitutes, and thieves whose lives, the Nation contended, were ethically impoverished by white racist neglect of their most fundamental needs: the need for self-respect, the need for social dignity, the need to understand their royal black history, and the need to worship and serve a black God. All of these were provided in the black nationalist worldview of the Nation of Islam.

Malcolm's public ministry of proselytizing for the Nation of Islam depended heavily on drawing contrasts between what he and other Nation members viewed as the corruption of black culture by white Christianity (best symbolized in Martin Luther King, Jr., and segments of the civil rights movement) and the redemptive messages of racial salvation proffered by Elijah Muhammad. Malcolm relentlessly preached the virtues of black self-determination and self-defense even as he denounced the brainwashing of black people by Christian preachers like King who espoused passive strategies of resistance in the face of white racist violence.

Where King advocated redemptive suffering for blacks through their own bloodshed, Malcolm promulgated "reciprocal bleeding" for blacks and whites. As King preached the virtues of Christian love, Malcolm articulated black anger with unmitigated passion. While King urged nonviolent civil disobedience, Malcolm promoted the liberation of blacks by whatever means were necessary, including (though not exclusively, as some have argued) the possibility of armed self-defense. While King dreamed, Malcolm saw nightmares.

It was Malcolm's unique ability to narrate the prospects of black resistance at the edge of racial apocalypse that made him both exciting and threatening. Malcolm spoke out loud what many blacks secretly felt about racist white people and practices, but were afraid to acknowledge publicly. Malcolm boldly specified in lucid rhetoric the hurts, agonies, and frustrations of black people chafing from an enforced racial silence about the considerable cultural costs of white racism.

Unfortunately, as was the case with most of his black nationalist compatriots and civil rights advocates, Malcolm cast black liberation in terms of masculine self-realization. Malcolm's zealous trumpeting of the social costs of black male cultural emasculation went hand in hand with his often aggressive, occasionally vicious, put-downs of black women. These slights of black women reflected the demonology of the Nation of Islam, which not only viewed racism as an ill from outside its group, but argued that women were a lethal source of deception and seduction from within. Hence, Nation of Islam women were virtually desexualized through "modest" dress, kept under the close supervision of men, and relegated to the background while their men took center stage. Such beliefs reinforced the already inferior position of black women in black culture.

These views, ironically, placed Malcolm and the Nation of Islam squarely within misogynist traditions of white and black Christianity. It is this aspect, especially, of Malcolm's public ministry that has been adopted by contemporary black urban youth, including rappers and filmmakers. Although Malcolm would near the end of his life renounce his sometimes vitriolic denunciations of black women, his contemporary followers have not often followed suit.

But as the civil rights movement expanded its influence, Malcolm and the Nation came under increasing criticism for its deeply apolitical stance. Officially, the Nation of Islam was forbidden by Elijah Muhammad to become involved in acts of civil disobedience or social protest, ironically containing the forces of anger and rage that Malcolm's fiery rhetoric helped unleash. This ideological constraint stifled Malcolm's natural inclination to action, and increasingly caused him great discomfort as he sought to explain publicly the glaring disparity between the Nation's aggressive rhetoric and its refusal to become politically engaged.

Malcolm's growing dissatisfaction with the Nation's apolitical posture only deepened his suspicions about its leadership role in aiding blacks to achieve real liberation. Malcolm also became increasingly aware of the internal corruption of the Nation—unprincipled financial practices among top officials who reaped personal benefit at the expense of the rank and file, and extramarital affairs involving leader Elijah Muhammad. Moreover, there is evidence that Malcolm had privately forsaken his belief in the whites-are-devils doctrine years before his widely discussed public rejection of the doctrine after his 1964 split from the Nation of Islam, his embrace of orthodox Islamic belief, and his religious pilgrimage to Mecca.[2]

The official cause of Malcolm's departure from the Nation of Islam was Elijah Muhammad's public reprimand of Malcolm for his famous comments that President John F. Kennedy's assassination merely represented the "chickens coming home to roost." Malcolm was saying that the violence the United States had committed in other parts of the world was returning to haunt this nation. Muhammad quickly forbade Malcolm from publicly speaking, initially for ninety days, motivated as much by jealousy of Malcolm's enormous popularity among blacks outside the Nation of Islam as by his desire to punish Malcolm for a comment that would bring the Nation undesired negative attention from an already racially paranoid government.

In March 1964, Malcolm left the Nation of Islam after it became apparent that he could not mend his relationship with his estranged mentor. He formed two organizations, one religious (Muslim Mosque) and the other political (Organization of Afro-American Unity, or OAAU). The OAAU was modeled after the Organization of African Unity and reflected Malcolm's belief that broad social engagement provided blacks their best chance for ending racism. Before establishing the OAAU, however, Malcolm fulfilled a long-standing dream of making a hajj to Mecca. While there, Malcolm wrote a series of letters to his followers detailing his stunning change of heart about race relations, declaring that his humane treatment by white Muslims and his perception of the universality of Islamic religious truth had forced him to reject his former narrow beliefs about whites. Malcolm's change of heart, though, did not blind him to the persistence of American racism and the need to oppose its broad variety of expressions with aggressive social resistance.

After his departure from the Nation of Islam, Malcolm traveled extensively, including trips to the Middle East and Africa. His travels broadened his political perspective considerably, a fact reflected in his new appreciation of socialist movements (though he didn't embrace socialism) and a new international note in his public discourse as he emphasized the link between African-American liberation and movements for freedom throughout the world, especially in African nations. Malcolm didn't live long enough to fulfill the promise of his new directions. On February 21, 1965, three months shy of his fortieth birthday, Malcolm X was gunned down by Nation of Islam loyalists as he prepared to speak to a meeting of the OAAU. Fortunately, Malcolm had recently completed his autobiography with the help of Alex Haley. That work, *The Autobiography of Malcolm X*, stands as a classic of black letters and American autobiography.[3]

Malcolm lived only fifty weeks after his break with the Nation of Islam, initiating his last and perhaps most meaningful transformation of all: from revolutionary black nationalist to human rights advocate. Although Malcolm never gave up on black unity or self-determination—and neither did he surrender his acerbic wit on behalf of the voiceless millions of poor blacks who could never speak their pain before the world—he did expand his field of vision to include poor, dispossessed people of color from around the world, people whose plight resulted from class inequality and economic oppression as much as from racial domination. Had he lived, we can only hope that vexing contemporary problems from gender oppression to homophobia might have exercised his considerable skills of social rage and incisive, passionate oratory in giving voice to fears and resentments that most people can speak only in private.

During the last year of his life, Malcolm's social criticism and political engagement reflected a will to spontaneity, his analysis an improvisatory and fluid affair that drew from his rapidly evolving quest for the best means available for real black liberation—but a black liberation connected to the realization of human rights for all suffering peoples. In the end, Malcolm's moral pragmatism and experimental social criticism linked him more nearly to the heart of African-American culture and American radical practices than it might have otherwise appeared during his controversial career. Malcolm's complexity resists neat categories of analysis and rigid conclusions about his meaning.

It is this Malcolm—the Malcolm who spoke with uncompromising ardor about the poor, black, and dispossessed, and who named racism when and where he found it—who appealed to me as a young black male coming to maturity during the 1970s in the ghetto of Detroit. I took pleasure in his early moniker Detroit Red, feeling that our common geography joined us in a project to reclaim the dignity of black identity from the chaotic dissemblances and self-deceptions instigated by racist oppression.

But the riots of 1967—with their flames of frustration burning bitterly in my neighborhood, a testament to the unreconciled grievances that fueled racial resentments—had already confirmed Malcolm's warnings about the desperate state of urban black America. And the death of Martin Luther King, Jr., one year later ruptured the veins of nonviolent response to black suffering, evoking seizures of social unrest in the nerve centers of hundreds of black communities across the nation. King's death and Malcolm's life forced me to grapple with the best remedy for resisting racism.

As a result, I turned more frequently to a means of communication and combat that King and Malcolm had favored and that had been nurtured in me by my experience in the black church: rhetorical resistance. In African-American cultures, acts of rhetorical resistance are often more than mere words. They encompass a complex set of symbolic expressions and oral interactions with the "real" world. These expressions and interactions are usually supported by substantive black cultural traditions—from religious worship to social protest—that fuse speech and performance. Much of the ingenuity and inventiveness of black rhetorical resistance was evident in the church-based civil rights movement and in black nationalist struggles for self-determination in the 1960s.

One form of rhetorical resistance that has been prominently featured throughout black cultural history is the black sermon, the jewel in the crown of black sacred rhetoric. Here, a minister, or another authorized figure, thrives in the delivery of priestly wisdom and prophetic warning through words of encouragement and comfort, of chastening and challenge. Martin and Malcolm, of course, were widely acknowledged masters of black sacred rhetoric—as well as brilliant political rhetoricians whose deft weaving of spiritual uplift and secular complaint forged a powerful basis for black action in a bruising white world. The excellent examples of Martin and Malcolm—along with the more immediate impact of my pastor, Frederick G. Sampson—brought me to believe that words can have world-making and life-altering consequences.

In the years following Malcolm's and Martin's deaths, I participated in all manner of black public oral performance—from church plays and speeches to poetry recitations and oratorical contests—that whetted my appetite for the word. At eleven, I wrote a speech for the local Optimist Club that won me a first-place trophy and a photograph and headline in the *Detroit News* that read "Boy's Plea Against Racism Wins Award." Martin's and Malcolm's spirit hovered intimately around my performance. Their presence in word also inspired my decision to become an ordained Baptist minister, and sustained me as I became, in quick succession, a teen-age father, a welfare recipient, a wheel-brake-and-drum-factory laborer, and a pastor in the South.

As I have matured, journeying from factory worker to professor, it is the Malcolm who valued truth over habit who has appealed most to me, his ability to be self-critical and to change his direction an unfailing sign of integrity and courage. But these two Malcolms need not be in ultimate, fatal conflict, need not be fractured by the choice between seeking an empowering racial identity and linking ourselves to the truth no matter what it looks like, regardless of color, class, gender, sex, or age. They are both legitimate quests, and Malcolm's career and memory are enabling agents for both pursuits. His complexity is our gift.

PART I
MALCOLM X'S
INTELLECTUAL
LEGACY

If I say, my father was Betty Shabazz's lawyer, the
poem can go no further. I've given you the punchline.
If you know who she is, all you can think about is how
and what you want to know about me, about my father,
about Malcolm, especially in 1990 when he's all over t-
shirts and medallions, but what I'm telling you is that
Mrs. Shabazz was a nice lady to me, and I loved her
name for the wrong reasons, SHABAZZ! and what I
remember is going to visit her daughters in 1970 in a
dark house with little furniture and leaving with a
candy necklace the daughters gave me, to keep. Now that
children see his name and call him, Malcolm Ten, and
someone called her Mrs. Ex-es, and they don't really
remember who he was or what he said or how he smiled
the way it happened when it did, and neither do I, I
think about how history is made more than what happened
and about a nice woman in a dark house filled with
daughters and candy, something dim and unspoken,
expectation.

Elizabeth Alexander, "What I'm Telling You"

2
X MARKS THE PLOTS: A CRITICAL READING OF MALCOLM'S READERS

> I think all of us should be critics of each other. Whenever you can't stand criticism you can never grow. I don't think that it serves any purpose for the leaders of our people to waste their time fighting each other needlessly. I think that we accomplish more when we sit down in private and iron out whatever differences that may exist and try and then do something constructive for the benefit of our people. But on the other hand, I don't think that we should be above criticism. I don't think that anyone should be above criticism.
>
> Malcolm X, in *Malcolm X: The Last Speeches*

The life and thought of Malcolm X have traced a curious path to black cultural authority and social acceptance since his assassination in 1965. At the time of his martyrdom—achieved through a murder that rivaled in its fumbling but lethal execution the treacherous twists of a Shakespearean tragedy—Malcolm was experiencing a radical shift in the personal and political understandings that governed his life and thought.[1] Malcolm's death heightened the confusion that had already seized his inner circle because of his last religious conversion. His death also engendered bitter disagreement among fellow travelers about his evolving political direction, conflicts that often traded on polemic, diatribe, and intolerance. Thus Malcolm's legacy was severely fragmented, his contributions shredded in ideological disputes even as ignorance and fear ensured his further denigration as the symbol of black hatred and violence.

Although broader cultural investigation of his importance has sometimes flagged, Malcolm has never disappeared among racial and political subcultures that proclaim his heroic stature because he embodied ideals of black rebellion and revolutionary social action.[2] The contemporary revival of black nationalism, in particular, has focused renewed attention on him. Indeed, he has risen to a black cultural stratosphere that was once exclusively occupied by Martin Luther King, Jr. The icons of success that mark Malcolm's ascent—ranging from posters, clothing, speeches, and endless sampling of his voice on rap recordings—attest to his achieving the pinnacle of his popularity more than a quarter century after his death.

Malcolm, however, has received nothing like the intellectual attention devoted to Martin Luther King, Jr., at least nothing equal to his cultural significance. Competing waves of uncritical celebration and vicious criticism—which settle easily into myth and caricature—have undermined appreciation of Malcolm's greatest accomplishments. The peculiar needs that idolizing or demonizing Malcolm fulfill mean that intellectuals who study him are faced with the difficult task of describing and explaining a controversial black leader and the forces that produced him.[3] Such critical studies must achieve the "thickest description" possible of Malcolm's career while avoiding explanations that either obscure or reduce the complex nature of his achievements and failures.[4]

Judging by these standards, the literature on Malcolm X has often missed the mark. Even the classic *Autobiography of Malcolm X* reflects both Malcolm's need to shape his personal history for public racial edification while bringing coherence to a radically conflicting set of life experiences and coauthor Alex Haley's political biases and ideological purposes.[5] Much writing about Malcolm has either lost its way in the murky waters of psychology dissolved from history or simply substituted—given racial politics in the United States—defensive praise for critical appraisal. At times, insights on Malcolm have been tarnished by insular ideological arguments that neither illuminate nor surprise. Malcolm X was too formidable a historic figure—the movements he led too variable and contradictory, the passion and intelligence he summoned too extraordinary and disconcerting—to be viewed through a narrow cultural prism.

My intent in this chapter is to provide a critical path through the quagmire of conflicting views of Malcolm X. I have identified at least four Malcolms who emerge in the intellectual investigations of his life and career: Malcolm as hero and saint, Malcolm as a public moralist, Malcolm as victim and vehicle of psychohistorical forces, and Malcolm as revolutionary figure judged by his career trajectory from nationalist to alleged socialist. Of course, many treatments of Malcolm's life and thought transgress rigid boundaries of interpretation. The Malcolms I have identified, and especially the categories of interpretation to which they give rise, should be viewed as handles on broader issues of ideological warfare over who Malcolm is, and to whom he rightfully belongs. In short, they help us answer Whose Malcolm is it?

I am not providing an exhaustive review of the literature, but a critical reading of the dominant tendencies in the writings on Malcolm X.[6] The writings make up an intellectual universe riddled with philosophical blindnesses and ideological constraints, filled with problematic interpretations, and sometimes brimming with brilliant insights. They reveal as much about the possibilities of understanding and explaining the life of a great black man as they do about Malcolm's life and thought.

A Critical Reading of Malcolm's Readers

Hero Worship and the Construction of a Black Revolutionary

In the tense and confused aftermath of Malcolm's death, several groups claiming to be his ideological heirs competed in a warfare of interpretation over Malcolm's torn legacy. The most prominent of these included black nationalist and revolutionary groups such as the Student Nonviolent Coordinating Committee (SNCC, under the leadership of Stokely Carmichael), the Congress of Racial Equality (CORE, under the leadership of James Farmer and especially Floyd McKissick), the Black Panther party, the Republic of New Africa, and the League of Revolutionary Black Workers.[7] They appealed to his vision and spirit in developing styles of moral criticism and social action aimed at the destruction of white supremacy. These groups also advocated versions of Black Power, racial self-determination, black pride, cultural autonomy, cooperative socialism, and black capitalism.[8]

Malcolm's death also caused often bitter debate between custodians of his legacy and his detractors, either side arguing his genius or evil in a potpourri of journals, books, magazines, and newspapers. For many of Malcolm's keepers, the embrace of his legacy by integrationists or Marxists out to re-create Malcolm in their distorted image was more destructive than his critics characterizing him in exclusively pejorative terms.

For all his nationalist followers, Malcolm is largely viewed as a saintly figure defending the cause of black unity while fighting racist oppression. Admittedly, the development of stories that posit black heroes and saints serves a crucial cultural and political function. Such stories may be used to combat historical amnesia and to challenge the deification of black heroes—especially those deemed capable of betraying the best interests of African-Americans—by forces outside black communities. Furthermore, such stories reveal that the creation of (black) heroes is neither accidental nor value neutral, and often serves political ends that are not defined or controlled by black communities. Even heroes proclaimed worthy of broad black support are often subject to cultural manipulation and distortion.

The most striking example of this involves Martin Luther King, Jr. Like Malcolm X, King was a complex historic figure whose moral vision and social thought evolved over time.[9] When King was alive, his efforts to effect a beloved community of racial equality were widely viewed as a threat to a stable social order. His advocacy of nonviolent civil disobedience was also viewed as a detrimental detour from the proper role that religious leaders should play in public. Of course, the rise of black radicalism during the late 1960s softened King's perception among many whites and blacks. But King's power to excite the social imagination of Americans only increased after his assassination.

The conflicting uses to which King's memory can be put—and the obscene manner in which his radical legacy can be deliberately forgotten—are displayed in aspects of the public commemoration of his birthday. To a significant degree, perceptions of King's public aims have been shaped by the corporate sector and (sometimes hostile) governmental forces. These forces may be glimpsed in Coca-Cola commercials celebrating King's birthday, and in Ronald Reagan's unseemly hints of King's personal and political defects at the signing of legislation to establish King's birthday as a national holiday.

King's legacy is viewed as most useful when promoting an unalloyed optimism about the possibilities of American social transformation, which peaked during his "I Have a Dream" speech. What is not often discussed—and is perhaps deliberately ignored—is how King dramatically revised his views, glimpsed most eloquently in his Vietnam-era antiwar rhetoric and in his War-on-Poverty social activism. Corporation-sponsored commercials that celebrate King's memory—most notably, television spots by McDonald's and Coca-Cola aimed at connecting their products to King's legacy—reveal a truncated understanding of King's meaning and value to American democracy. These and other efforts at public explanation of King's meaning portray his worth as underwriting the interests of the state, which advocates a distorted cultural history of an era actually shaped more by blood and brutality than by distant dreams.

Many events of public commemoration avoid assigning specific responsibility for opposition to King's and the civil rights movement's quest for equality. On such occasions, the uneven path to racial justice is often described in a manner that makes progress appear an inevitable fact of our national life. Little mention is made of the concerted efforts—not only of bigots and white supremacists, but, more important, of government officials and average citizens—to stop racial progress. Such stories deny King's radical challenge to narrow conceptions of American democracy. Although King and other sacrificial civil rights participants are lauded for their possession of the virtue of courage, not enough attention is given to the vicious cultural contexts that called forth such heroic action.

Most insidious of all, consent to these whitewashed stories of King and the 1960s is often secured by the veiled threat that King's memory will be either celebrated in this manner or forgotten altogether. The logic behind such a threat is premised on a belief that blacks should be grateful for the state's allowing King's celebration to occur at all. These realities make the battle over King's memory—waged by communities invested in his radical challenge to American society—a constant obligation. The battle over King's memory also provides an important example to communities interested in preserving and employing Malcolm's memory in contemporary social action. As with King, making Malcolm X a hero reveals the political utility of memory and reflects a deliberate choice made by black communities to identify and honor the principles for which Malcolm lived and died.

For many adherents, Malcolm remained until his death a revolutionary black nationalist whose exclusive interest was to combat white supremacy while fostering black unity. Although near the end of his life Malcolm displayed a broadened humanity and moral awareness—qualities overlooked by his unprincipled critics and often denied by his true believers—his revolutionary cohorts contended that Malcolm's late-life changes were cosmetic and confused, the painful evidence of ideological vertigo brought on by paranoia and exhaustion.

All these interpretations are vividly elaborated in John Henrik Clarke's anthology *Malcolm X: The Man and His Times*.[10] Clarke's book brings together essays, personal reflections, interviews, and organizational statements that provide a basis for understanding and explaining different dimensions of Malcolm's life and career. Although its various voices certainly undermine a single understanding of Malcolm's meaning as a father, leader, friend, and husband (after all, it includes writers as different as Albert Cleage and Gordon Parks), the book's tone suggests an exercise in hero worship and saint making, as cultural interpreters gather and preserve fragments of Malcolm's memory.

Thus even the power of an individual essay to critically engage an aspect of Malcolm's contribution or failure is overcome by the greater urgency of the collective enterprise: to establish Malcolm as a genuine hero of the people, but more than this, a sainted son of revolutionary struggle who was perfectly fit for the leadership task he helped define. But moments of criticism come through. For instance, in the course of a mostly favorable discussion of Malcolm's leadership, Charles Wilson insightfully addresses the structural problems confronting black protest leaders as he probes Malcolm's "failure of leadership style and a failure to evolve a sound organizational base for his activities," concluding that Malcolm was a "victim of his own charisma."[11]

At least two other writers in the collection also attempt to critically explore Malcolm's limitations and the distortions of his legacy by other groups. James Boggs deplores both the racism of white Marxist revolutionaries who cannot see beyond color and the lack of "scientific analysis" displayed by Malcolm's black nationalist heirs whose activity degenerates into Black Power sloganeering. And Wyatt Tee Walker, King's former lieutenant, criticizes Malcolm for "useless illogical and intemperate remarks that helped neither him nor his cause," while emphasizing the importance of Malcolm's pro-black rhetoric and his promulgation of the right to self-defense.[12] At the same time, Walker uselessly repeats old saws about the vices of black matriarchy.

But these flutters of criticism are mostly overridden by the celebrative and romantic impulses that are expressed in several essays. Fortunately, Patricia Robinson's paean to Malcolm X as a revolutionary figure stops short of viewing black male patriarchy as a heroic achievement. Instead, she sees Malcolm as the beginning of a redeemed black masculinity that helps, not oppresses, black children and women. But in essays by W. Keorapetse Kgositsile, Abdelwahab M. Elmessiri, and Albert Cleage, Malcolm's revolutionary black nationalist legacy is almost breathlessly, even reverentially, evoked.

Cleage especially, in his "Myths About Malcolm X," seeks to defend Malcolm's black nationalist reputation from assertions that he was becoming an integrationist, an internationalist, or a Trotskyist Marxist, concluding that "if in Mecca he had decided that blacks and whites can unite, then his life at that moment would have become meaningless in terms of the world struggle of black people."[13] Clarke's book makes sense, especially when viewed against the historical canvas of late-1960s racial politics and in light of the specific cultural needs of urban blacks confronting deepening social crisis after Malcolm's death. But its goal of redeeming Malcolm's legacy through laudatory means makes its value more curatorial than critical.

Similarly, Oba T'Shaka's *The Political Legacy of Malcolm*

X is an interpretation of Malcolm X as a revolutionary black nationalist, and *The End of White World Supremacy: Four Speeches by Malcolm X*, edited by Benjamin Karim, attempts to freeze Malcolm's development in the fateful year before his break with Elijah Muhammad and the Nation of Islam.[14] T'Shaka is an often perceptive social critic and political activist who believes that "the scattering of Africans throughout the world gave birth to the idea of Pan-Africanism," and that the "oppression of Blacks in the United States cannot be separated from the oppression of Africans on the African continent and in the world."[15]

Such an international perspective establishes links between blacks throughout the world, forged by revolutionary black nationalist activity expressed in political insurgency, material and resource sharing, and the exchange of ideas. In this context, T'Shaka maintains that Malcolm was a revolutionary black nationalist who "identified the world-wide system of white supremacy as the number one enemy of Africans and people of color throughout the world." He argues that Malcolm's internationalist perspective on revolutionary political resistance was specifically linked to African experiments in socialist politics, contending that Malcolm rejected European models of political transformation. Not surprisingly, T'Shaka is sour on the notion that after his trip to Mecca Malcolm accepted and expressed support for black–white unity, and he characterizes beliefs that Malcolm began to advocate a Trotskyite social-ism as "farfetched statements."[16]

Although he gives a close reading of Malcolm's ideas, T'Shaka's treatment of Malcolm is marred by largely un-critical explorations of Malcolm's rhetoric. He fails to chal-lenge Malcolm's philosophical presuppositions or even critically to juxtapose contradictory elements of Malcolm's rhetoric. In effect, he bestows a canonical cloak on Mal-colm's words. Nor does T'Shaka give a persuasive expla-nation of the social forces and political action that shaped Malcolm's thinking in his last years. Understanding these facts might illuminate the motivation behind Malcolm's utopian interpretations of black separatist ideology, which maintained that racial division was based on blacks pos-sessing land either in Africa or in the United States. Al-though T'Shaka, following Malcolm's own schema, draws distinctions between his long-range program (that is, return to Africa, which he claims Malcolm never gave up) and short-term tactics (that is, cultural, psychological, and phil-osophical migration), he doesn't prove that Malcolm ever resolved the ideological tensions in black nationalism.

Karim's *The End of White World Supremacy* is an attempt to wrench Malcolm's speeches from their political context and place them in a narrative framework that uses Mal-colm's own words—even after his break with the Nation of Islam—to justify Elijah Muhammad's religious theodicy.

Such a move ignores Malcolm's radically transformed self-understanding and asserts, through his own words, a world-view he eventually rejected. Karim, who as Benjamin Goodman was Malcolm's close associate through his Nation of Islam phase until his death, says in his introduction that Muhammad gave Malcolm "the keys to knowledge and understanding," that this is "one key point in Malcolm's life that is still generally misunderstood, or overlooked," and that these speeches "represent a fair cross section of his teaching during that crucial last year as a leader in the Nation of Islam."[17]

Karim's introduction to the speeches winks away the ideological warfare that helped drive Malcolm from the Nation of Islam, and ignores evidence that Malcolm grew to characterize his years with Muhammad as "the sickness and madness of those days."[18] Here we have Malcolm the master polemicist telling twice-told tales of Mr. Yacub and white devils, a doctrine he had long forsaken. Here, too, is Malcolm the skillful dogmatist deriding Paul Robeson for not knowing his history, when in reality Malcolm grew to admire Robeson and tried to meet him a month before his own death.[19] The political context Karim gives to the speeches attempts to transform interesting and essential historical artifacts from Malcolm's past into a living document of personal faith and belief.

Karim's shortcomings reveal the futility of examining

A Critical Reading of Malcolm's Readers

Malcolm's life and thought without regard for sound historical judgment and intellectual honesty. Serious engagement with Malcolm's life and thought must be critical and balanced. The most useful evaluations of Malcolm X are those anchored in forceful but fair criticism of his career that hold him to the same standards of scholarly examination as we would any figure of importance to (African-) American society. But such judgments must acknowledge the tattered history of vicious, uncomprehending, and disabling cultural criticism aimed at black life, a variety of criticism reflected in many cultural commentaries on Malcolm's life.[20]

The overwhelming weakness of hero worship, often, is the belief that the community of hero worshipers possesses the *definitive* understanding of the subject—in this instance, Malcolm—and that critical dissenters from the received view of Malcolm are traitors to black unity, inauthentic heirs to his political legacy, or misguided interpreters of his ideas.[21] This is even more reason for intellectuals to bring the full weight of their critical powers to bear on Malcolm's life. Otherwise, his real brilliance will be diminished by efforts to canonize his views without first considering them, his ultimate importance as a revolutionary figure sacrificed to celebratory claims about his historic meaning. Toward this end, Malcolm's words best describe the critical approach that should be adopted in examining his life and thought:

Now many Negroes don't like to be criticized—they don't like for it to be said that we're not ready. They say that that's a stereotype. We have assets—we have liabilities as well as assets. And until our people are able to . . . analyze ourselves and discover our own liabilities as well as our assets, we never will be able to win any struggle that we become involved in. As long as the black community and the leaders of the black community are afraid of criticism and want to classify all criticism, collective criticism, as a stereotype, no one will ever be able to pull our coat. . . . [W]e have to . . . find out where we are lacking, and what we need to replace that which we are lacking, [or] we never will be able to be successful.[22]

The Vocation of a Public Moralist

Within African-American life, a strong heritage of black leadership has relentlessly and imaginatively addressed the major obstacles to the achievement of a sacred trinity of social goods for African-Americans: freedom, justice, and equality. Racism has been historically viewed as the most lethal force to deny black Americans their share in the abundant life that these goods make possible. The central role that the church has traditionally played in many black communities means that religion has profoundly shaped the moral vision and social thought of black leaders' responses to racism.[23] Because freedom, justice, and equality have been viewed by black communities as fundamental in the exercise of citizenship rights and the expression of social dignity, a diverse group of black leaders has advocated varied models of racial transformation in public life.

The centrality of Christianity in African-American culture means that the moral character of black public protest against racism has oscillated between reformist and revolutionary models of racial transformation. From Booker T. Washington to Joseph H. Jackson, black Christian reformist approaches to racial transformation have embraced liberal notions of the importance of social stability and the legitimacy of the state. Black Christian reformist leaders have sought to shape religious resistance to oppression, inequality, and injustice around styles of rational dissent that reinforce a stable political order. From Nat Turner to the latter-day Martin Luther King, Jr., black Christian revolutionary approaches to racial transformation have often presumed the fundamental moral and social limitations of the state. Black Christian revolutionary leaders have advocated public protest against racism in a manner that disrupts the forceful alliance of unjust social privilege and political legitimacy that have undermined African-American life.

In practice, black resistance to American racism has fallen somewhere between these two poles. At their best, black leaders have opposed American racism while appealing to religion and politics in prescribing a remedy. Whether influenced by black Christianity, Black Muslim belief, or other varieties of black religious experience, proponents of public morality combined spiritual insight with political resistance in the attempt to achieve social reconstruction. Any effort to understand Malcolm X, and the cultural and religious beliefs he appealed to and argued against in making his specific claims, must take these traditions of prophetic and public morality into consideration.

Of the four books that largely view Malcolm's career through his unrelenting ethical insights and the moral abominations to which his vision forcefully responded, Louis Lomax's *When the Word Is Given: A Report on Elijah Muhammad, Malcolm X, and the Black Muslim World* and James Cone's *Martin and Malcolm and America: A Dream or a Nightmare?* treat the religious roots of Malcolm's moral vision. Peter Goldman's *The Death and Life of Malcolm X* and Lomax's *To Kill a Black Man* expound the social vision and political implications of Malcolm's moral perspective. Moreover, both Lomax's and Cone's books are comparative studies of Malcolm and Martin Luther King, Jr., Malcolm's widely perceived ideological opposite. The pairing of these figures invites inquiry about the legitimacy and usefulness of such comparisons, questions I will take up later.[24]

Lomax's *When the Word Is Given* is a perceptive and informal ethnography of the inner structure of belief of the Nation of Islam, a journalist's attempt to unveil the mysterious concatenation of religious rituals, puritanical behavior, and unorthodox beliefs that have at once intimidated and intrigued outsiders. Although other, more scholarly critics have examined Black Muslim belief, Lomax is a literate amateur whose lucid prose and imaginative reporting evoke the electricity and immediacy of the events he describes.[25]

Lomax is also insightful in his description of the cultural forces that helped bring Black Muslim faith into existence. He artfully probes how the Nation of Islam proved essential during the 1950s and 1960s for many black citizens who were vulnerably perched at the crux of the racial dilemma in the United States, seeking psychic and social refuge from the insanity of the country's fractured urban center. In Lomax's portrait, it is at the juncture between racist attack and cultural defense that Malcolm X's moral vocation emerges: he voices the aspirations of the disenfranchised, the racially displaced, the religiously confused, and the economically devastated black person. As Lomax observes, the "Black Muslims came to power during a moral interregnum"; Malcolm "brings his message of importance and dignity to a class of Negroes who have had little, if any, reason to feel proud of themselves as a race or as individuals."[26]

Despite the virtue of including several of Malcolm's speeches and interviews, which compose the second half of the book (including an interview during Malcolm's suspension from the Nation), the study's popular purposes largely stifle a sharp analysis of Malcolm's moral thought. Lomax provides helpful historical background of the origins and evolution of the Black Muslim worldview, linking useful insights on the emergence of religion in general to Islamic and Christian belief in Africa and in the United States. But his study does not engage the contradictions of belief and ambiguities of emotion that characterized Malcolm's moral life. In fairness to Lomax, this study was not his final word on Malcolm. But his later comparative biography of Malcolm and King is more striking for its compelling personal insight into two tragic, heroic men than for its comprehension of the constellation of cultural factors that shaped their lives.

Cone's *Martin and Malcolm and America*, on the contrary, is useful precisely because it explores the cultural, racial, and religious roots of Malcolm's public moral thought.[27] Cone, the widely acknowledged founder of black theology, has been significantly influenced by both King and Malcolm, and his book is a public acknowledgment of intellectual debt and personal inspiration. In chapters devoted to the impact of Malcolm's northern ghetto origins on his later thought, the content of his social vision, and the nature of his mature reflections on American society and black political activity, Cone discusses Malcolm's understanding of racial oppression, social justice, black unity, self-love, separatism, and self-defense that in the main constituted his vision of black nationalism.[28]

Cone performs a valuable service by shedding light on Malcolm's religious faith and then linking that faith to his social ideals and public moral vision, recognizing that his faith "was marginal not only in America as a whole but in the African-American community itself."[29] Cone covers familiar ground in his exposition of Malcolm's views on white Americans, black Christianity, and the religious and moral virtues of Elijah Muhammad's Black Muslim faith. But he also manages to show how Malcolm's withering criticisms of race anticipated "the rise of black liberation theology in the United States and South Africa and other expressions of liberation theology in the Third World."[30]

The most prominent feature of Cone's book is its comparative framework, paralleling and opposing two seminal influences on late-twentieth-century American culture. It is just this presumption—that Malcolm and Martin represented two contradictory, if not mutually exclusive, ideological options available to blacks in combating the absurdity of white racism—that generates interest in Cone's book, and in Lomax's *To Kill a Black Man*.[31] But is this presumption accurate?

As with all strictly imagined oppositions, an either–or division does not capture what Ralph Ellison termed the "beautiful and confounding complexities of Afro-American culture.''[32] Nor does a rigid dualism account for the fashion in which even sharp ideological differences depend on some common intellectual ground to make disagreement plausible. For instance, the acrimonious ideological schism between Booker T. Washington and W. E. B. Du Bois drew energy from a common agreement that something must be done about the black cultural condition, that intellectual investigation must be wed to cultural and political activity in addressing the various problems of black culture, and that varying degrees of white support were crucial to the attainment of concrete freedom for black Americans.[33] Although Washington is characterized as an ''accommodationist'' and Du Bois as a ''Pan-African nationalist,'' they were complex human beings whose political activity and social thought were more than the sum of their parts.

The comparative analysis of King and Malcolm sheds light on the strengths and weaknesses of the public-moralist approach to Malcolm's life and career. By comparing the two defining figures of twentieth-century black public morality, we are allowed to grasp the experienced, lived-out distinctions between King's and Malcolm's approaches to racial reform and revolution. Because King and Malcolm represent as well major tendencies in historic black ideological warfare against white racism, their lives and thought are useful examples of the social strategies, civil rebellion, religious resources, and psychic maneuvers adopted by di-

Conclusion.

verse black movements for liberation within American society.

The challenge to the public-moralist approach is to
probe the sort of tensions between King and Malcolm that
remain largely unexplored by other views of either figure.
For instance, it is the presence of class differences within
black life that bestowed particular meanings on King's
and Malcolm's leadership. Such differences shaped the
styles each leader adapted in voicing the grievances of his
constituency—for King, a guilt-laden, upwardly mobile,
and ever-expanding black middle class; for Malcolm, an   *lead*
ever-widening, trouble-prone, and rigidly oppressed black
ghetto poor. These differences reflect deep and abiding
schisms within African-American life that challenge facile
or pedestrian interpretations of black leaders, inviting instead complex theoretical analyses of their public moral language and behavior.

The comparison of King and Malcolm may also, ironically, void the self-critical dimensions of the public-moralist
perspective, causing its proponents to leave unaddressed,
for instance, the shortcomings of a sexual hierarchy of social
criticism in black life. Although Cone is critical of Malcolm's
and Martin's failures of sight and sense on gender issues,
more is demanded. What we need is an explanation of how
intellectuals and leaders within vibrant traditions of black
social criticism seem, with notable exception, unwilling or

unable to include gender difference as a keyword in their public-moralist vocabulary. A comparative analysis of King and Malcolm may point out how *they* did not take gender difference seriously, but it does not explain how the public-moralist traditions in which they participated either enabled or prevented them from doing so.

By gaining such knowledge, we could determine if their beliefs were representative of their traditions, or if other participants (for example, Douglass and Du Bois, who held more enlightened views on gender) provide alternative perspectives from which to criticize Malcolm and Martin without resorting to the fingerpointing that derives from the clear advantage of historical hindsight.

As Cone makes clear, Malcolm and Martin were complex political actors whose thought derived from venerable traditions of response to American racism, usefully characterized as nationalism and integrationism. But as Cone also points out, the rhetoric of these two traditions has been employed to express complex beliefs, and black leaders and intellectuals have often combined them in their struggles against slavery and other forms of racial oppression.

Lomax, by comparison, more rigidly employs these figures to "examine the issues of 'integration versus separation,' 'violence versus nonviolence,' 'the relevance of the Christian ethic to modern life,' and the question 'can American institutions as now constructed activate the self-corrective power that is the basic prerequisite for racial harmony?' "[34] Lomax is most critical of Malcolm, leading one commentator to suggest that Lomax's assessment of Malcolm betrayed their friendship.[35] Lomax points out the wrongheadedness of Malcolm's advocacy of violence, the contradictions of his ideological absolutism, and the limitations of his imprecisely formulated organizational plans in his last year. His criticisms of King, however, are mostly framed as the miscalculations of strategy and the failure of white people to justify King's belief in them. Lomax's vision of Malcolm loses sight of the formidable forces that were arrayed against him, and the common moral worldviews occupied by King and his white oppressors, which made King's philosophical inclinations seem natural and legitimate, and Malcolm's, by that measure, foreign and unacceptable. One result of Lomax's lack of appreciation for this difference is his failure to explore King's challenge to capitalism, a challenge that distinguished King from Malcolm for most of Malcolm's career.

Another problem is that we fail to gain a more profitable view of Malcolm's real achievements, overlooking the strengths and weaknesses of the moral tradition in which he notably participated. Malcolm was, perhaps, the living indictment of a white American moral worldview. But his career was the first fruit as well of something more radical: an alternative racial cosmos where existing moral principles are viewed as the naked justification of power and thought to be useless in illumining or judging the propositions of an authentically black ethical worldview. Not only did Malcolm call for the rejection of particular incarnations of moral viewpoints that have failed to live up to their own best potential meanings (a strategy King employed to brilliant effect), but, given how American morality is indivisible from the network of intellectual arguments that support and justify it, he argued for the rejection of American public morality itself. Malcolm lived against the fundamental premises of American public moral judgment: that innocence and corruption are on a continuum, that justice and injustice are on a scale, and that proper moral choices reflect right decisions made between good and evil within the given moral outlook.

Malcolm's black Islamic moral criticism posed a significant challenge to its black Christian counterpart, which has enjoyed a central place in African-American culture. Malcolm challenged an assumption held by the most prominent black Christian public moralists: that the social structure of American society should be rearranged, but not reconstructed. Consequently, Malcolm focused a harshly critical light on the very possibility of interracial cooperation, common moral vision, and social coexistence.

A powerful vision of Malcolm as a public moralist can be seen in Goldman's *The Death and Life of Malcolm X*. Goldman captures with eloquence and imagination the Brobdingnagian forces of white racial oppression that made life hell for northern poor blacks, and the Lilliputian psychic resources apparently at their disposal before Malcolm's oversized and defiant rhetoric rallied black rage and anger to their defense. Goldman's Malcolm is one whose "life was itself an accusation—a passage to the ninth circle of that black man's hell and back—and the real meaning of his ministry, in and out of the Nation of Islam, was to deliver that accusation to us." Malcolm was a "witness for the prosecution" of white injustice, a "public moralist." With each aspect of Malcolm's life that he treats—whether his anticipation of Black Power or his capitulation to standards of moral evaluation rooted in the white society he so vigorously despised—Goldman's narrative skillfully defends the central proposition of Malcolm's prophetic public moral vocation.[36]

Goldman's book is focused on Malcolm's last years before his break with Muhammad, and tracks Malcolm's transformation after Mecca. Goldman contends that this transformation occurred as process, not revelation, and that it ran over weeks and months of trial and error, discovery, disappointment. Additionally, Goldman sifts through the conflicting evidence of Malcolm's assassination.[37] Goldman maintains that only one of Malcolm's three convicted and imprisoned assassins is justly jailed, and that two other murderers remain free.[38] Goldman says about Malcolm's Organization of Afro-American Unity (OAAU), which he founded in his last year, that its "greatest single asset was its star: its fatal flaw was that it was constructed specifically as a star vehicle for a man who didn't have the time to invest in making it go."[39]

When it was written in 1973, and revised in 1979, Goldman's was the only full-length biography of Malcolm besides Lomax's *To Kill a Black Man*. The virtue of Goldman's book is that it taps into the sense of immediacy that drives Lomax's book, while also featuring independent investigation of Malcolm's life through more than a hundred interviews with Malcolm himself. Goldman's treatment of Malcolm also raises a question that I will more completely address later: Can a white intellectual understand and explain black experience? Goldman's book helps expose the cultural roots and religious expression of Elijah Muhammad's social theodicy, an argument Malcolm took up and defended with exemplary passion and fidelity. He describes Malcolm's public moral mission to proclaim judgment on white America with the same kind of insight and clarity that characterized many of Malcolm's public declarations.

Explaining Malcolm as a public moralist moves admirably beyond heroic reconstruction to critical appreciation. The significance of such an approach is its insistence on viewing Malcolm as a critical figure in the development of black nationalist repudiations of white cultural traditions, economic practices, and religious institutions. And yet, unlike hero worshipers who present treatments of Malcolm's meaning, the authors who examine the moral dimensions of Malcolm's public ministry are unafraid to be critical of his ideological blindnesses, his strategic weakness, his organizational limitations, and his sometimes bristling moral contradictions.

But if they display an avidity, and aptitude, for portraying Malcolm's moral dimensions and the forces that made his vision necessary, Malcolm's public-moralist interpreters have not as convincingly depicted the forces that make public morality possible. The public-moralist approach is almost by definition limited to explaining Malcolm in terms of the broad shifts and realignment of contours created within the logic of American morality itself, rarely asking whether public moral proclamation and action are the best means of effecting social revolution. This approach largely ignores the hints of rebellion against capitalist domination contained in Malcolm's latest speeches, blurring as well a focus on King's mature beliefs that American society was "sick" and in need of a "reconstruction of the entire society, a revolution of values."[40]

This approach also fails to place Malcolm in the intricate nexus of social and political forces that shaped his career as a religious militant and a revolutionary black nationalist. It does not adequately convey the mammoth scope of economic and cultural forces that converged during the 1940s, 1950s, and 1960s, not only shaping the expression of racial domination, but influencing as well patterns of class antagonism and gender oppression. As Clayborne Carson argues in his splendid introduction to the FBI files on Malcolm X, most writings have failed to "study him within the context of American racial politics during the 1950s and 1960s."[41] According to Carson, the files track Malcolm's growth from the "narrowly religious perspective of the Nation of Islam toward a broader Pan-Africanist worldview," shed light on his religious and political views and the degree to which they "threatened the American state," and "clarif[y] his role in modern African-American politics."[42]

Moreover, the story of Malcolm X and the black revolution he sought to effect is also the story of how such social aspirations were shaped by the advent of nuclear holocaust in the mid-1940s (altering American ideals of social stability and communal life expectation), the repression of dissident speech in the 1950s under the banner of McCarthyism, and the economic boom of the mid-1960s that contrasted starkly to shrinking resources for the black poor. A refined social history not only accents such features, but provides as well a complex portrait of Malcolm's philosophical and political goals, and the myriad factors that drove or denied their achievement.

Malcolm's most radical and original contribution rested in reconceiving the possibility of being a worthful black human being in what he deemed a wicked white world. He saw black racial debasement as the core of an alternative moral sphere that was justified for no other reason than its abuse and attack by white Americans. To understand and explain Malcolm, however, we must wedge beneath the influences that determined his career in learning how his public moral vocation was both necessary and possible.

Psychobiography and the Forces of History

If the task of biography is to help readers understand human action, the purpose of psychobiography is to probe the relationship between psychic motivation, personal behavior, and social activity in explaining human achievement and failure. The project to connect psychology and biography grows out of a well-established quest to merge various schools of psychological theory with other intellectual disciplines, resulting in ethnopsychiatry, psychohistory, social psychology, and psychoanalytic approaches to philosophy.[43]

Behind the turn toward psychology and social theory by biographers is a desire to take advantage of the insight yielded from attempts to correlate or synthesize the largely incompatible worlds of psychoanalysis and Marxism carved out by Freud and Marx and their unwieldy legion of advocates and interpreters. If one argues, however, as Richard Lichtman does, that "the structure of the two theories makes them ultimate rivals," then, as he concedes, "priorities must be established."[44] In his analysis of the integration of psychoanalysis into Marxist theory, Lichtman argues that "working through the limitations of Freud's view makes its very significant insights available for incorporation into an expanded Marxist theory."[45]

Psychobiographers have acknowledged the intellectual difficulties to which Lichtman points while using Marxist or Freudian theory (and sometimes both) to locate and illumine gnarled areas of human experience. For instance, Erik Erikson's *Gandhi's Truth: On the Origins of Militant Nonviolence*, one of psychobiography's foundational works, weds critical analysis of its subject's cultural and intellectual roots to imaginative reflections on the sources of Gandhi's motivation, sacrifice, and spiritual achievement.[46]

As they bring together social and psychological theory in their research, psychobiographers often rupture the rules that separate academic disciplines. Then again, if the psychobiographer is ruled by rigid presuppositions and is insensitive to the subject of study, nothing can prevent the results from being fatally flat. Two recent psychobiographies of Malcolm X reveal that genre's virtues and vices.

Eugene Victor Wolfenstein's *The Victims of Democracy: Malcolm X and the Black Revolution* is a work of considerable intellectual imagination and rigorous theoretical insight.[47] It takes measure of the energies that created Malcolm and the demons that drove him. Wolfenstein assesses Malcolm's accomplishments through a theoretical lens as noteworthy for its startling clarity about Malcolm the individual as for its wide-angled view of the field of forces with which Malcolm contended during his childhood and mature career.

Wolfenstein uses an elaborate conceptual machinery to examine how racism falsifies "the consciousness of the racially oppressed," and how racially oppressed individuals struggle to "free themselves from both the falsification of their consciousness and the racist domination of their practical activity."[48] For Wolfenstein's purpose, neither a psychoanalytic nor a Marxist theory alone could yield adequate insight because Freudianism "provides no foundation for the analysis of interests, be they individual or collective," and Marxism "provides no foundation for the analysis of desires." Therefore, a "unifying concept of human nature was required."[49]

Wolfenstein's psychobiography is especially helpful because it combines several compelling features: a historical analysis of the black (nationalist) revolutionary struggle, an insightful biographical analysis of Malcolm X's life, and an imaginative social theory that explains how a figure like Malcolm X could emerge from the womb of black struggle against American apartheid. Wolfenstein accounts for how Malcolm's childhood was affected by violent, conflicting domestic forces and describes how black culture's quest for identity at the margins of American society—especially when viewed from the even more marginal perspective of the black poor—shaped Malcolm's adolescence and young adulthood.

Wolfenstein also explores Malcolm's career as a zealous young prophet and public mouthpiece for Elijah Muhummad, revealing the psychic and social needs that Malcolm's commitments served. Wolfenstein's imaginative remapping of Malcolm's intellectual and emotional landscape marks a significant contribution as well to the history of African-American ideas, offering new ways of understanding one of the most complex figures in our nation's history.

Undoubtedly, Wolfenstein's book would have benefited from a discussion of how black religious groups provided social and moral cohesion in northern urban black communities, and from a description of their impact on Earl Little's ministry. Although Wolfenstein perceptively probes the appeal of Marcus Garvey's Universal Negro Improvement Association to blacks—and the social, psychological, and economic ground it partly shared with the Ku Klux Klan and white proletarian workers—his psychoanalytic Marxist interpretation of Earl Little and Malcolm would have been substantially enhanced by an engagement with black Protestant beliefs about the relationship between work, morality, and self-regard.[50]

Wolfenstein is often keenly insightful about black liberation movements and the forces that precipitated their eruption, but his dependence on biological definitions of race weakens his arguments.[51] The value of more complex readings of race is that they not only show how the varied meanings of racism are created in society; but prove as well that the idea of race has a cultural history.[52] More complex theories of race would permit Wolfenstein to illumine the changing intellectual and social terrain of struggle by groups that oppose the vicious meanings attributed to African-American identity by cultural racists.

In the end, Wolfenstein is too dependent on the revelations and reconstructions of self-identity that Malcolm (with Haley's assistance) achieved in his autobiography. In answering his own rhetorical questions about whether Malcolm and Haley represented Malcolm accurately, Wolfenstein says that from a "purely empirical standpoint, I believe the answer to both questions is generally affirmative."[53] The problem, of course, is that Malcolm's recollections are not without distortions. These distortions, when taken together with the book's interpretive framework, not only reveal his attempts to record his life history, but reflect as well his need to control how his life was viewed during the ideological frenzy that marked his last year. By itself, self-description is an unreliable basis for reconstructing the meaning of Malcolm's life and career. Still, Wolfenstein's work is the most sophisticated treatment to date of Malcolm's intellectual and psychological roots.

But Bruce Perry's uneven psychobiographical study, *Malcolm: The Life of a Man Who Changed Black America*, which reaches exhaustively beyond Malcolm's self-representation in his autobiography, possesses little of the psychoanalytic rigor and insight of Wolfenstein's work.[54] Although Perry unearths new information about Malcolm, he does not skillfully clarify the impact that such information should have on our understanding of Malcolm. The volume renders Malcolm smaller than life.

In Perry's estimation, Malcolm's childhood holds the interpretive key to understanding his mature career as a black leader: Malcolm's "war against the white power structure evolved from the same inner needs that had spawned earlier rebellions against his teachers, the law, established religion, and other symbols of authority."[55] Perry's picture of Malcolm's family is one of unremitting violence, criminality, and pathology. The mature Malcolm is equally tragic: a man of looming greatness whose self-destruction "contributed to his premature death."[56] It is precisely here that Perry's psychobiography folds in on itself, its rough edges puncturing the center of its explanatory purpose. It is not that psychobiography cannot remark on the unraveling of domestic relations that weave together important threads of personal identity, threads that are also woven into adolescent and adult behavior. But Perry has a penchant for explaining complex psychic forces—and the social conditions that influence their makeup—in simplistic terms and tabloid-like arguments.

Still, Perry's new information about Malcolm is occasionally revealing, though some of the claims he extracts from this information are more dubious than others. When, for instance, Perry addresses areas of Malcolm's life that can be factually verified, he is on solid ground. By simply checking Malcolm's school records Perry proves that, contrary to his autobiography, Malcolm was not expelled from West Junior High School but actually completed the seventh grade in 1939. And by interviewing several family members, Perry establishes that neither Malcolm's half-sister Ella nor his father, Earl, were, as Malcolm contended, "jet black," a claim Perry views as Malcolm's way of equating "blackness and the strength his light-skinned mother had lacked."[57] Despite Malcolm X's assertion of close friendships with Lionel Hampton, Sonny Greer, and Cootie Williams during his hustling days, Perry's interviews show that the "closeness Malcolm described was as fictitious as the closeness he said he had shared with the members of his own family."[58]

But when Perry addresses aspects of Malcolm's experience that invite close argument and analytical interpretation, he is on shakier ground. At this juncture, Perry displays an insensitivity to African-American life and an ignorance about black intellectual traditions that weaken his book. For instance, Perry depicts Malcolm's travels to Africa—partially in an attempt to expand his organization's political and financial base, but also to express his increasingly international social vision—as intended solely to fund his fledgling organization. Perry also draws questionable parallels between the cloudy events surrounding a fire at Malcolm's family farm during his early childhood in 1929 (which Perry concludes points to arson by Earl Little) and the fire at Malcolm's New York house after his dispute with Nation of Islam officials over ownership rights.

A major example of the limitation of Perry's psycho-biographical approach is his treatment of Malcolm's alleged homosexual activity, both as an experimenting adolescent and as a hustling, income-seeking young adult. Perry's remarks are more striking for the narrow assumptions that underlie his interpretations than for their potential to dismantle the quintessential symbol of African-American manhood. If Malcolm did have homosexual relations, they might serve Perry as a powerful tool of interpretation to expose the tangled cultural roots of black machismo, and to help him explain the cruel varieties of homophobia that afflict black communities. A complex understanding of black sexual politics challenges a psychology of masculinity that views "male" as a homogeneous, natural, and universally understood identity. A complex understanding of masculinity maintains that male identity is also significantly affected by ethnic, racial, economic, and sexual differences.

But Perry's framework of interpretation cannot assimilate the information his research has unearthed. Although the masculinist psychology that chokes much of black leadership culture needs to be forcefully criticized, Perry's observations do not suffice. Because he displays neither sensitivity to nor knowledge about complex black cultural beliefs regarding gender and sexual difference, Perry's portrait of Malcolm's sex life forms a rhetorical low blow, simply reinforcing a line of attack against an already sexually demonized black leadership culture.

The power of psychobiography in discussing black leaders is its potential to shed light on its subjects in a manner that traditional biography fails to achieve. African-American cultural studies, which has traditionally made little use of psychoanalytic theory, has sacrificed the insights such an undertaking might offer while avoiding the pitfalls of psychological explanations of human motivation. After all, psychobiography is also prone to overreach its capacity to explain.

In some ways, the psychobiographer's quest for (in this case) the "real Malcolm" presumes that human experience is objective and that truth is produced by explaining the relation between human action and psychic motivation. Such an approach may seduce psychobiographers into believing that they are gaining access to the static, internal psychic reality of a historical figure. Often such access is wrongly believed to be separate from the methods of investigation psychobiographers employ, and from the aims and presumptions, as well as the biases and intellectual limitations, that influence their work.

Because both Wolfenstein and Perry (like Goldman) are white, their psychobiographies in particular raise suspicion about the ability of white intellectuals to interpret black experience. Although such speculation is rarely systematically examined, it surfaces as both healthy skepticism and debilitating paranoia in the informal debates that abound in a variety of black intellectual circles. Such debates reflect two crucial tensions generated by psychobiographical explanations of black leaders by white authors: that such explanations reflect insensitivity to black culture, and that white proponents of psychobiographical analysis are incompetent to assess black life adequately. Several factors are at the base of such conclusions.

First is the racist history that has affected every tradition of American scholarship and that has obscured, erased, or distorted accounts of the culture and history of African-Americans.[59] Given this history (and the strong currents of anti-intellectualism that flood most segments of American culture), suspicion of certain forms of critical intellectual activity survive in many segments of black culture. Also, black intellectuals have experienced enormous difficulty in securing adequate cultural and financial support to develop self-sustaining traditions of scholarly investigation and communities of intellectual inquiry.[60]

For example, from its birth in the womb of political protest during the late 1960s and early 1970s, black studies has been largely stigmatized and usually underfunded. Perhaps the principal reasons for this are the beliefs held by many whites (and some blacks) that, first, black scholars should master nonblack subjects, and second, that black studies is intellectually worthless. Ironically, once the more than 200 black studies programs in American colleges and universities became established, many white academics became convinced that blacks are capable of studying only "black" subjects.

At the same time, black studies experienced a new "invasion" by white intellectuals. This new invasion—mimicking earlier patterns of white scholarship on black life even as most black scholars were prevented from being published—provoked resentment from black scholars.[61] The resentment hinged on the difficulty black scholars experienced in securing appointments in most academic fields beyond black studies. Black scholars were also skeptical of the intellectual assumptions and political agendas of white scholars, especially because there was strong precedence for many white scholars to distort black culture in their work by either exoticizing or demonizing its expression. Black intellectual skeptics opposed to white interpretations of black culture and figures employ a variety of arguments in their defense.

Many black intellectuals contend that black experience is unique and can be understood, described, and explained only by blacks. Unquestionably, African-American history produces cultural and personal experiences that are distinct, even singular. But the *historical* character of such experiences makes them theoretically accessible to any interpreter who has a broad knowledge of African-American intellectual traditions, a balanced and sensible approach to black culture, and the same skills of rational argumentation and scholarly inquiry required in other fields of study.

There is no special status of being that derives from black cultural or historical experience that grants black interpreters an automatically superior understanding of black cultural meanings. This same principle allows black scholars to interpret Shakespeare, study Heisenberg's uncertainty principle, and master Marxist social theory. In sum, black cultural and historical experiences do not produce ideas and practices that are incapable of interpretation when the most critically judicious and culturally sensitive methods of intellectual inquiry are applied.

Many intellectuals also believe that black culture is unified and relatively homogeneous. But this contention is as misleading as the first, especially in light of black culture's wonderful complexity and radical diversity. The complexity and diversity of black culture means that a bewildering variety of opinions, beliefs, ideologies, traditions, and practices coexist, even if in a provisional sort of way. Black conservatives, scuba divers, socialists, and rock musicians come easily to mind. All these tendencies and traditions constitute and help define black culture. Given these realities, it is pointless to dismiss studies of black cultural figures *simply* because their authors are white. One must judge any work on African-American culture by standards of rigorous critical investigation while attending to both the presuppositions that ground scholarly perspectives and the biases that influence intellectual arguments.

Psychobiographies of Malcolm X's life and career represent an important advance in Malcolm studies. The crucial issue is not color, but consciousness about African-American culture, sensitivity to trends and developments in black society, knowledge of the growing literature about various dimensions of black American life, and a theoretical sophistication that artfully blends a variety of disciplinary approaches in yielding insight about a complex historic figure like Malcolm X. When psychobiography is employed in this manner, it can go a long way toward breaking new ground in understanding and explaining the life of important black figures. When it is incompetently wielded, psychobiographical analysis ends up simply projecting the psychobiographer's intellectual biases and limitations of perspective onto the historical screen of a black figure's career.

Voices in the Wilderness: Revolutionary Sparks and Malcolm's Last Year

To comprehend the full sweep of a figure's life and thought, it is necessary to place that figure's career in its cultural and historical context and view the trends and twists of thought that mark significant periods of change and development.

Such an approach may be termed a trajectory analysis because it attempts to outline the evolution of belief and thought of historic figures by matching previously held ideas to newer ones, seeking to grasp whatever continuities and departures can be discerned from such an enterprise. Trajectory analysis, then, may be a helpful way of viewing a figure such as Martin Luther King, Jr., whose career may be divided into the early optimism of civil rights ideology to the latter-day aggressive nonviolence he advocated on the eve of his assassination. It may also be enlightening when grappling with the serpentine mysteries of Malcolm's final days.

Malcolm's turbulent severance from Elijah Muhammad's psychic and world-making womb initiated yet another stage of his personal and political evolution, marking a conversion experience. On one level, Malcolm freed himself from Elijah's destructive ideological grip, shattering molds of belief and practice that were no longer useful or enabling. On another level, Malcolm's maturation and conversion were the result of his internal ideals of moral expectation, social behavior, and authentic religious belief. His conversion, though suddenly manifest, was most likely a gradual process involving both conscious acts of dissociation from the Nation of Islam and the "subconscious incubation and maturing of motives deposited by the experiences of life."[62]

Many commentators have heavily debated the precise

nature of Malcolm's transformation. Indeed, his last fifty weeks on earth form a fertile intellectual field where the seeds of speculation readily blossom into conflicting interpretations of Malcolm's meaning at the end of his life. Lomax says that Malcolm became a "lukewarm integrationist."[63] Goldman suggests that Malcolm was "improvising," that he embraced and discarded ideological options as he went along.[64] Cleage and T'Shaka hold that he remained a revolutionary black nationalist. And Cone asserts that Malcolm became an internationalist with a humanist bent.

But the most prominent and vigorous interpreters of the meaning of Malcolm's last year have been a group of intellectuals associated with the Socialist Workers Party, a Trotskyist Marxist group that took keen interest in Malcolm's post-Mecca social criticism and sponsored some of his last speeches. For the most part, their views have been articulately promoted by George Breitman, author of *The Last Year of Malcolm X: The Evolution of a Revolutionary* and editor of two volumes of Malcolm's speeches, organizational statements, and interviews during his last years: *Malcolm X Speaks: Selected Speeches and Statements* and *By Any Means Necessary: Speeches, Interviews, and a Letter, by Malcolm X*. A third volume of Malcolm's speeches, *Malcolm X: The Last Speeches*, was edited by Bruce Perry, who claimed ideological difference with the publisher.[65]

Breitman's *The Last Year of Malcolm X* is a passionately argued book that maintains Malcolm's split with Elijah took

Malcolm by surprise, making it necessary for him to gain time and experience to reconstruct his ideological beliefs and redefine his organizational orientation. Breitman divides Malcolm's independent phase into two parts: the transition period, lasting the few months between his split in March 1964 and his return from Africa at the end of May 1964; and the final period, lasting from June 1964 until his death in February 1965. Breitman maintains that in the final period, Malcolm "was on the way to a synthesis of black nationalism and socialism that would be fitting for the American scene and acceptable to the masses in the black ghetto."[66]

For Breitman's argument to be persuasive, it had to address Malcolm's continuing association with a black nationalism that effectively excluded white participation, or else show that he had developed a different understanding of black nationalism. Also, he had to prove that Malcolm's anticapitalist statements and remarks about socialism represented a coherent and systematic exposition of his beliefs as a political strategist and social critic. Breitman contends that in the final period, Malcolm made distinctions between separatism (the belief that blacks should be socially, culturally, politically, and economically separate from white society) and nationalism (the belief that blacks should control their own culture).

Malcolm's views of nationalism changed after his encounters with revolutionaries in Africa who were "white," however, and in his "Young Socialist" interview in *By Any Means Necessary,* Malcolm confessed that he had "had to do a lot of thinking and reappraising" of his definition of black nationalism.[67] Breitman argues that though he "had virtually stopped calling himself and the OAAU black nationalist," because others persisted in the practice, he accepted "its continued use in discussion and debate."[68] Malcolm said in the same interview, "I haven't been using the expression for several months."[69]

But how can Breitman then argue that Malcolm was attempting a synthesis of black nationalism and socialism if the basis for Malcolm's continued use of the phrase "black nationalism" was apparently more convenience and habit than ideological conviction? What is apparent from my reading of Malcolm's speeches is that his reconsideration of black nationalism occurred amid a radically shifting worldview that was being shaped by events unfolding on the international scene and by his broadened horizon of experience. His social and intellectual contact with activists and intellectuals from several African nations forced him to relinquish the narrow focus of his black nationalist practice and challenged him to consider restructuring his organizational base to reflect his broadened interests.

If, therefore, even Malcolm's conceptions of black nationalist strategy were undergoing profound restructuring, it is possible to say only that his revised black nationalist ideology *might* have accommodated socialist strategy. It is equally plausible to suggest that his nationalist beliefs might have collapsed altogether under the weight of apparent ideological contradictions introduced by his growing appreciation of class and economic factors in forming the lives of the black masses.[70] For the synthesis of black nationalism and socialism that Breitman asserts Malcolm was forging to have been plausible, several interrelated processes needed to be set in motion.

First, for such a synthesis to have occurred, a clear definition of the potential connection of black nationalism and socialism was needed. The second need was for a discussion of the ideological similarities and differences between the varieties of black nationalism and socialism to be joined. And the third need was for an explicit expression of the political, economic, and social interests that an allied black nationalism and socialism would mutually emphasize and embrace; the exploration of intellectual and political problems both would address; and an identification of the common enemies both would oppose. But given the existential and material matters that claimed his rapidly evaporating energy near the end of his life, Malcolm hardly had the wherewithal to perform such tasks.

Breitman also maintains that Malcolm's final period marked his maturation as "a revolutionary—increasingly anti-capitalist and pro-socialist as well as anti-imperialist," labels that Breitman acknowledges Malcolm himself never adopted.[71] Breitman reads Malcolm's two trips to Africa as a time of expansive political reeducation, when Malcolm gained insight into the progressive possibilities of socialist revolutionary practice. After his return to the United States from his second trip, Malcolm felt, Breitman says, the need to express publicly his "own anti-capitalist and pro-socialist convictions," which had "become quite strong by this time."[72] He cites interviews and speeches Malcolm made during this period to substantiate his claim, including Malcolm's speaking at the Audubon Ballroom on December 20, 1964, of how almost "every one of the countries that has gotten independence has devised some kind of socialist system, and this is no accident."[73]

Such a strategy, one that seeks to predict probable ideological and intellectual outcomes, may shed less light on Malcolm than is initially apparent. Breitman's contention that Malcolm was becoming a socialist; Cleage's that he was confused; T'Shaka's that he maintained a vigorous revolutionary black nationalist stance; and Goldman's that he was improvising can all be proclaimed and documented with varying degrees of evidence and credibility.

This is not to suggest that one view is as good as the next or that they are somehow interchangeable, because we are uncertain about Malcolm's final direction. It simply suggests that the nature of Malcolm's thought during his last year was ambiguous and that making definite judgments about his direction is impossible. In this light, trajectories say more about the ideological commitments and intellectual viewpoints of interpreters than the objective evidence evoked to substantiate claims about Malcolm's final views.

The truth is that we have only a bare-bones outline of Malcolm's emerging worldview. In "The Harlem 'Hate-Gang' Scare," contained in *Malcolm X Speaks* (and delivered during what Breitman says was Malcolm's final period), Malcolm says that during his travels he

> noticed that most of the countries that had recently emerged into independence have turned away from the so-called capitalistic system in the direction of socialism. So out of curiosity, I can't resist the temptation to do a little investigating wherever that particular philosophy happens to be in existence or an attempt is being made to bring it into existence.[74]

But at the end of his speech, in reply to a question about the kind of political and economic system that Malcolm wanted, he said, "I don't know. But I'm flexible. . . . As was stated earlier, all of the countries that are emerging today from under the shackles of colonialism are turning toward socialism."[75]

This tentativeness is characteristic of Malcolm's

speeches throughout the three collections that contain fragments of his evolving worldview, especially *Malcolm X Speaks* and *By Any Means Necessary*. Even the speeches delivered during his final period showcase a common feature: Malcolm displays sympathy for and interest in socialist philosophy without committing himself to its practice as a means of achieving liberation for African-Americans.

Malcolm confessed in the "Young Socialist" interview, "I still would be hard pressed to give a specific definition of the overall philosophy which I think is necessary for the liberation of the black people in this country."[76] Of course, as Breitman implies, Malcolm's self-description is not the only basis for drawing conclusions about his philosophy. But even empirical investigation fails to yield conclusive evidence of his social philosophy because it was in such radical transformation and flux.

Malcolm was indeed improvising from the chords of an expanded black nationalist rhetoric and an embryonic socialist criticism of capitalist civilization. Although Breitman has been maligned as a latecomer seeking to foist his ideological beliefs onto Malcolm's last days, there is precedence for Trotskyist attempts to address the problem of racism and black nationalism in the United States.[77] And the venerable black historian C. L. R. James became a Marxist, in part, by reading Trotsky's *History of the Russian Revolution*.[78] Although Malcolm consistently denounced capitalism, he did not live long enough to embrace social-ism.

The weakness of such an interpretive trajectory, then, is that it tends to demand a certainty about Malcolm that is clearly unachievable. An ideological trajectory of Malcolm's later moments is forced to bring coherence to fragments of political speech more than systematic social thought, to ex-aggerate moments of highly suggestive ideological gestures rather than substantive political activity, and to focus on slices of organizational breakthrough instead of the complex integrative activity envisioned for the OAAU. In the end, it is apparent that Malcolm was rapidly revising his worldview as he experienced a personal, religious, and ideological con-version that was still transpiring when he met his brutal death.

But the thrust behind such speculation is often a focus on how Malcolm attempted to shape the cultural forces of his time through the agency of moral rhetoric, social criti-cism, and prophetic declaration. Just as important, but often neglected in such analyses, is an account of how Malcolm was shaped by his times, of how he was the peculiar and particular creation of black cultural forces and American social practices. Armed with such an understanding, the fo-cus on Malcolm's last year would be shifted away from sim-ply determining what he said and did to determining how we should use his example to respond to our current cul-tural and national crises.

In the Prison of Prisms:
The Future of Malcolm's Past

The literature on Malcolm X is certain to swell with the
renewed cultural interest in his life. And although the particular incarnations of the approaches I have detailed may
fade from intellectual view or cultural vogue, the ideological
commitments, methodological procedures, historical perspectives, cultural assumptions, religious beliefs, and philosophical presuppositions they employ will most assuredly
be expressed in one form or another in future treatments
of his life and thought.[79]

The canonization of Malcolm will undoubtedly continue. Romantic and celebratory treatments of his social action and revolutionary rhetoric will issue forth from black
intellectuals, activists, and cultural artists. This is especially
true in the independent black press, where Malcolm's memory has been heroically kept alive in books, pamphlets, and
magazines, even as his presence receded from wide visibility
and celebration before his recent revival. The independent
black press preserves and circulates cultural beliefs, intellectual arguments, and racial wisdom among black folk
away from the omniscient eye and acceptance of mainstream publishing.

Shahrazad Ali's controversial book, *The Blackman's
Guide to Understanding the Blackwoman,* for instance, sold hundreds of thousands of copies without receiving much atten-

tion from mainstream newspapers, magazines, or journals. The mainstream press often overlooked Malcolm's contributions, but black publications like *The Amsterdam News*, *The Afro-American*, *Bilalian News*, and *Black News* scrupulously recorded his public career. The black independent press, in alliance with various black nationalist groups throughout the country that have maintained Malcolm's heroic stature from the time of his assassination, is a crucial force in Malcolm's ongoing celebration. Such treatments of his legacy will most likely be employed by these groups to actively resist Malcolm's symbolic manipulation by what they understand to be the forces of cultural racism, state domination, commodification, and especially religious brainwashing that Malcolm detested and opposed.

The enormous influence of the culture of hip-hop on black youth, coupled with the resurgence of black cultural nationalism among powerful subcultures within African-America, suggests that Malcolm's heroic example will continue to be emulated and proclaimed. The stakes of hero worship are raised when considering the resurgent racism of American society and the increased personal and social desperation among the constituency for whom Malcolm eloquently argued, the black ghetto poor. Heightened racial antipathy in cultural institutions such as universities and businesses, and escalated attacks on black cultural figures, ideas, and movements, precipitate the celebration of figures who embody the strongest gestures of resistance to white racism.

Moreover, the destructive effects of gentrification, economic crisis, and social dislocation; the expansion of corporate privilege; and the development of underground political economies—along with the violence and criminality they breed—means that Malcolm is even more a precious symbol of the self-discipline, self-esteem, and moral leadership necessary to combat the spiritual and economic corruption of poor black communities. With their efforts to situate him among the truly great in African-American history, hero worshipers' discussion of Malcolm will be of important but limited value in critically investigating his revolutionary speech, thought, and action.

Malcolm's weaknesses and strengths must be rigorously examined if we are to have a richly hued picture of one of the most intriguing figures of twentieth-century public life in the United States. Malcolm's past is not yet settled, savaged as it has been in the embrace of unprincipled denigrators while being equally smothered in the well-meaning grip of romantic and uncritical loyalists. He deserves what every towering and seminal figure in history should receive: comprehensive and critical examination of what he said and did so that his life and thought will be useful to future generations of peoples in struggle around the globe.

MALCOLM X'S INTELLECTUAL LEGACY

As the cadre of Malcolm scholars expands, Malcolm's relation to black nationalism must be explored, especially because its themes and goals occupied so much of his life and thought. I will now turn to a discussion of how Malcolm's renewed popularity is wedded to a resurgence of black nationalist sentiment. The strengths of black nationalism, and its limitations and contradictions as well, serve to magnify Malcolm's achievements and failures alike.

PART II
MALCOLM X IN CONTEMPORARY SOCIETY

X

Everything we dont understand
     is explained
     in Art
     The Sun
     beats inside us
     The Spirit courses in and out

A circling transbluesency
     pumping Detroit Red inside, deep thru us
     like a Sea
          & who calls us bitter
          has bitten us
          & from that wound
               pours Malcolm
               Little
               by
               Little''

                    Amiri Baraka

3
MALCOLM X AND THE RESURGENCE OF BLACK NATIONALISM

And in my opinion the young generation of whites, blacks, browns, whatever else there is, you're living at a time of extremism, a time of revolution, a time when there's got to be a change. People in power have misused it, and now there has to be a change and a better world has to be built, and the only way it's going to be built is with extreme methods. I for one will join in with anyone, I don't care what color you are, as long as you want to change this miserable condition that exists on this earth.

Malcolm X, in *By Any Means Necessary: Speeches, Interviews, and a Letter,* by Malcolm X

Because Malcolm X for the duration of his life and most of his death occupied the shadowy periphery of black cultural politics—subsisting as the suppressed premise of the logic of black bourgeois resistance to racism—his reemergence as a cultural hero is something of a paradox. His newly acclaimed status is indivisible from the renaissance of black nationalism and owes as much to his overhauled heroism as to his commodification by black and white cultural entrepreneurs. I will explore Malcolm's brand of black nationalism while evaluating his use as a powerful icon in contemporary black nationalism. I will end with a brief reflection on his possible use in a program of progressive black politics.

Given this nation's racist legacy, it is no surprise that black folk have at every crucial juncture of their history in the United States expressed nationalist sentiment.[1] The peculiar social, economic, and political constraints of oppression, stretching from slavery to the present day, have always precipitated varying degrees of resistance, revolt, rebellion, or resentment from African-Americans. If nationalism is viewed as an attempt to establish and maintain a nation's identity, growing out of circumstances of social and cultural conflict, then black nationalism is a response of racial solidarity to the divisive practices of white supremacist nationalism.

Black nationalism has also been viewed as a response to the erosion of communal identity and the eradication of collective self-determination under slavery, and as a strategy to combat the destructive cultural effects resulting from the rejection of fragile black political liberties after Emancipation and Reconstruction. Black nationalism was often an expression of healthy self-regard in a legal and social climate that reinforced black Americans' inferior political status. Unlike many other expressions of nationalism, however, black nationalism was coerced from the beginning into a parasitic relationship to American culture. This confounding irony of black nationalist discourse and practice haunts it to this day.

Black nationalism is often contrasted to liberal integrationist ideology. Liberal integrationists believe that the goal of African-American struggles for liberation ought to be the inclusion of blacks in the larger compass of American social, political, and economic privilege, while maintaining a distinct appreciation for African-American culture. In its extreme expression, however, liberal integrationist ideology acquires a bland assimilationist emphasis. Racial assimilationists promote the uncritical adoption by blacks of the norms of civility, education, and culture nurtured in mainstream white American culture. Although overly sharp distinctions between forms of nationalism and integrationism are problematic (the two ideologies often coexist in a figure's thought or at different periods in an institution's or organization's life), comparing them can be helpful in capturing the two primary ideological thrusts in African-American communities.

The most prominent recent phase of black nationalist activity, prior to its contemporary resurgence, lasted from 1965 until 1973, from the emergence of Stokely Carmichael as leader of the Black Power movement, until the demise of the Black Panthers.[2] This period saw major black organizations denying whites participation in radical civil rights organizations like the Student Nonviolent Coordinating

Committee, the advocacy by black nationalist leaders of armed self-defense against racist state repression in the form of the police and the National Guard, the end of the powerful leadership of Malcolm X with his assassination in 1965, the bold articulation of black theology from James Cone in 1969, and the revolutionary insurgence planned and partially implemented by the Black Panthers.[3]

The cultural rebirth of Malcolm X, then, is the remarkable result of complex forces converging to lift him from his violent death in 1965. His heroic status hinges partially on the broad, if belated, appeal of his variety of black nationalism to Americans who, when he lived, either ignored or despised him. But Malcolm's appeal is strongest among black youth between the ages of fifteen and twenty-four, who find in him a figure of epic racial achievement.[4]

Rap culture, especially, has had a decisive influence in promoting Malcolm as a cultural hero. Because of the issues it addresses, and the often militant viewpoints it espouses, rap has often served as the popular cultural elaboration of certain features of Malcolm's legacy. The obstacles that rap has overcome in establishing itself as a mainstay of American popular culture—connected primarily to its style of expression and its themes—provide a natural link between Malcolm's radical social vocation and aspects of black youth culture. The similarity between aspects of hip-hop culture and Malcolm's public career (for example, charges of violence, the problems associated with expressing black rage and experiences in the ghetto, the celebration of black pride and historical memory) prods rappers to take the lead in asserting Malcolm's heroism for contemporary black America.

Rap music originated in the Bronx over a decade ago as urban teens experimented with various forms of cultural expression, from graffiti art to break dancing, creating art in the midst of the cultural and political invisibility to which they had been relegated. Rap was initially popular among black teens because of its staccato beats, its driving, lancing rhythms, and its hip lyrics, reflecting its origins in their world, a world that is increasingly an odyssey—through the terror of ghetto gangs, drugs, violence, and racism—in search of an authentic personal identity and legitimate social standing. The seemingly endless obstacles that frustrate this search, together with the humor, nonsense, and latent absurdity of some forms of urban life, provide the content of many rap songs.

Hip-hop began as an underground phenomenon, with artists such as Busy Bee, DJ Kool Hurk, Funky 4 Plus 1, Kurtis Blow, Kool Moe Dee, Afrika Bambaata, Cold Rush Brothers, and Grandmaster Melle Mel producing cassette tapes of their verbal play and distributing them from the trunks of cars, on street corners, and at neighborhood parties. In rap's initial phase, hip-hop artists usually applied their rhythmic skills by inserting words over music borrowed from popular 1970s R&B songs. For instance, hip-hop's breakthrough song, "Rapper's Delight," featured words added to the hit "Good Times," originally recorded by the R&B group Chic.

As rap evolved, it has largely proved to be a flexible musical form that experiments widely in order to reflect the varied visions of its creators. And like most black music before it, rap has escaped classification and ghettoization as a transient "black" fad and garnered mainstream attention. The fate of rap as a "legitimate" contender for mainstream acceptance was tied initially to the fortunes of the rap group Run-D.M.C. It produced the first rap album to be certified gold (500,000 copies sold), the first rap song to be featured on MTV, and the first rap album—"Raising Hell"—to go triple platinum (3 million copies sold). Run-D.M.C.'s crossover appeal was secured with its rap version of the white rock group Aerosmith's 1970s song "Walk This Way."

Since Run-D.M.C.'s epochal success, rap has exploded all previous predictions of its cultural and commercial appeal, nearly becoming a billion-dollar industry. And the recent rise to popularity of the controversial gangsta' rap—in which rappers employ guns, violence, and drugs as metaphors for cultural creativity, personal agency, and social criticism—has only increased the visibility and demonization of black youth culture. From socially conscious rap to hardcore hip-hop, from pop rappers to black nationalist groups, rap has easily become, with country music, the most popular form of musical expression during the 1990s.

One of the most obvious and starkly compelling features of rap culture is its form, drawing from an oral tradition with deep roots in African-American culture.[5] The tradition is one that Malcolm brilliantly participated in, relishing his capacity to verbally outfox his opponents with a well-placed word or a cleverly engineered rebuke. His broad familiarity with the devices of African-American oral culture—the saucy put-down, the feigned agreement turned to oppositional advantage, the hyperbolic expression generously employed to make a point, the fetish for powerful metaphor—marks his public rhetoric.

The hip-hop generation has appropriated Malcolm with unequaled passion, pushed along by the same affection for the word that drove him to read voraciously and speak with eloquence. Malcolm is the rap revolution's rhetorician of choice, his words forming the ideological framework for authentic black consciousness.[6] His verbal ferocity has been combined with the rhythms of James Brown and George Clinton, the three figures forming a trio of griots dispensing cultural wisdom harnessed to polyrhythmic beats.

Malcolm's public career, too, is the powerful if perplexing story of a series of personal and intellectual changes, a constellation of complicated and sometimes conflicting identities, that mark his evolution of thought, foreshadowing the perennial transformations of style and theme that characterize contemporary hip-hop. As rapper Michael Franti, says:

The thing I gained from him is not his symbol as a militant, but his ongoing examination of his life and how he was able to think critically about himself and grow and change as he encountered new information. That's where I feel that we gain strength, through constantly conquering our own shortcomings, and questioning our beliefs.[7]

Furthermore, as in Malcolm's public rallies—which focused black rage on suitable targets, especially black bourgeois liberal leaders and white racists—the rap concert encourages the explicit articulation of black anger in public. And like the misconceptions that often prevailed about Malcolm's provocative statements about self-defense, perceptions about the automatic or inevitable link between rap and violence are often grounded in ignorance rather than critical investigation of hip-hop's words or deeds.

Because Malcolm, too, addressed with unexcelled clarity and moral suasion the predicament of the ghetto poor, he is a natural icon for rap culture. As rappers Ultramagnetic M.C.'s state:

Everybody still listens to Malcolm X. When he talks you can't walk away. The thing about X is that he attracted and still attracts the people who have given up and lives [sic] recklessly—the crowd that just don't care what's going on. Making a difference in these people's lives is truly the essence of Malcolm X.[8]

Rappers often point as well to Malcolm X's phrase "no sellout, no sellout, no sellout" as the touchstone of a black cultural consciousness intent on preserving the authenticity of black cultural expressions, and as the basis for a true black nationalism.[9] But what precisely about Malcolm's black nationalist beliefs is the basis of his revived American heroism, especially for black youth?

Malcolm's defiant expression of black rage has won him a new hearing among a generation of black youth whose embattled social status due to a brutally resurgent racism makes them sympathetic to his fiery, often angry rhetoric. Malcolm's take-no-prisoners approach to racial crisis appeals to young blacks disaffected from white society and alienated from older black generations whose contained style of revolt owes more to Martin Luther King, Jr.,'s nonviolent philosophy than to Malcolm's advocacy of self-defense.

Moreover, Malcolm's expression of black rage—which, by his own confession, tapped a vulnerability even in King—has been adopted by participants in the culture of hip-hop, who often reflect Malcolm's militant posture. These artists, as do many of their black peers, find in Malcolm's uncompromising rhetoric the confirmation of their instincts about the "permanence of American racism."[10] Also, Malcolm's ability to say out loud what many blacks could say only privately endeared him to blacks when he was alive, and explains his appeal to youth seeking an explicit articulation of anger at American racism and injustice.

Another feature of Malcolm's nationalism has cemented his heroic status among young blacks: his withering indictments of the limitations of black bourgeois liberalism, expressed most clearly in the civil rights protest against white racial dominance. Malcolm showed little tolerance for the strategies, tactics, and philosophy of nonviolence that were central to the civil rights movement led by Martin Luther King, Jr.[11] Further, King's limited successes in reaching those most severely punished by poverty only reinforced the value of Malcolm's criticism of civil rights ideology.

Malcolm's pointed denunciations of black liberal protest against white racism hinged on the belief that black people should maintain independence from the very people who had helped oppress them—white people. Black bourgeois liberal protest encouraged white cooperation in the struggle to secure the fragile gains for which civil rights groups aimed in their quest for social justice. As one rap group illumines Malcolm's appeal: "The reason why Malcolm X has an influence on today's youth is because his influence as a leader was certainly equal, if not better than Dr. Martin Luther King. Everybody still listens to Malcolm X."[12] Another rap group believes that the "legacy of Malcolm X is to provide a clear counterpoint to the non-violent/ passive resistance theme presented by Dr. Martin Luther King, Jr."[13] Malcolm's heroic appeal as a critic of black bourgeois protest of white racism is summarized by C. Eric Lincoln, who contends that the source of Malcolm's undying magnetism

> lies in the simple fact that we have not yet overcome.
> . . . For many of the kids in the ghetto we are right back
> where we were. The few advances that have been
> made have not reached them. So if we didn't make it
> with King, what have we to lose? We might as well
> make it with Malcolm.[14]

Malcolm's black nationalist ideology expressed an alternative black spirituality and religious worldview that provided bold relief to the ethic of love advocated in black Christian conceptions of social protest. Although this component of his thinking is linked to Malcolm's denunciation of black liberal protest philosophies and strategies, his alternative black spirituality was rooted in the religious worldview of the Nation of Islam and promoted a black public theodicy that demonized whites as unquestionably evil.[15] And although Malcolm's understanding of white racism was rooted in a theological vision that lent religious significance to the unequal relationship between whites and blacks, his colorful articulation of his beliefs in his public addresses forged the expression of a black public theodicy

with which even secular or non-Muslim blacks could identify.

Central to Malcolm's alternative black spirituality was
his rejection of the belief that black people should redeem
white people through black bloodshed, sacrifice, and suffering. "We don't believe that Afro-Americans should be
victims any longer," he said. "We believe that bloodshed is
a two-way street."[16] He also contended that not "a single
white person in America would sit idly by and let someone
do to him what we Black men have been letting others do
to us."[17]

Malcolm's theological premises—the underpinning of
his black public theodicy—forced him to the conclusion that
white violence must be met with intelligent opposition and
committed resistance, even if potentially violent means
must be adopted in self-defense against white racism. Although Malcolm would near the end of his life alter his
views and concede the humanity of whites and their potential for assistance, he maintained a strong philosophical
commitment to proclaiming the evil of white racism and to
detailing its lethal consequences in poor black communities.

A fundamental appeal of Malcolm's black nationalism,
and indeed a large part of the cultural crisis that has precipitated Malcolm's mythic return, is rooted in a characteristic
quest in black America: the search for a secure and empowering racial identity. That quest is perennially frustrated by
the demands of American culture to cleanse ethnic and

racial particularity at the altar of a superior American identity, substituting the terms of one strain of nationalism for the priorities of another.

By this common ritual of national identity, for instance, the Irish, Poles, Italians, and Jews have been absorbed into a universal image of common citizenship. But the transformation of black cultural identity is often poorly served by this process, impeded as much by the external pressures of racism and class prejudice as by internal racial resistance to an "inclusion" that would rob blacks of whatever power and privilege they already enjoy in their own domains.

As further testimony to the contemporary black quest for a secure racial identity, gusts of racial pride sweep across black America as scholars retrieve the lost treasures of an unjustly degraded African past. This quest continues a project of racial reclamation begun in earnest in the nineteenth century, but recast to fit the needs of end-of-the-century utopian nationalists, including followers of Louis Farrakhan and Leonard Jeffries, and proponents of certain versions of Afrocentrism.[18]

Louis Farrakhan has caused a firestorm of controversial reaction to his anti-Semitism and to his support of the content of racist, sexist, and homophobic remarks made by former aide Khalid Abdul Muhammad at an infamous speech at Kean College in 1993. Leonard Jeffries has gained wide attention because of his allegedly anti-Semitic remarks about Jews' financing of the slave trade and his allegedly bigoted beliefs that Italians and Jews had collaborated in Hollywood to stereotype and denigrate blacks.[19] Both Farrakhan and Jeffries are beloved and celebrated among many blacks, however, because they speak their truth to the white powers-that-be without fear of punishment or retaliation. And the Afrocentric movement has quickened the debate about multicultural education and cast a searching light on the intellectual blindness and racist claims of Eurocentric scholars, even as it avoids acknowledging the romantic features of its own household.[20]

Malcolm's unabashed love for black history, his relentless pedagogy of racial redemption through cultural consciousness and racial self-awareness, mesh effortlessly with black Americans' (especially black youths') recovery of their African roots. As rapper KRS-One summarized a crucial feature of Malcolm's legacy, black children will "come to know that they come from a long race and line of kings, queens and warriors," a knowledge that will make them "have a better feeling of themselves."[21]

Perhaps above all other facets of Malcolm's heroic stature is his unfettered championing of the politics of black masculinity (a theme I will pursue more fully in the next chapter). Few other aspects of Malcolm's rejuvenated appeal have been as prominently invoked as Malcolm's focus on the plight and place of black men in American society. In light of the contemporary cultural status of black men, particularly young black males, it is easy to comprehend his heroic status as a defender of black men.

Although established black males like Bill Cosby, Michael Jordan, and Bryant Gumbel enjoy enormous success and broad acceptance because of their superior talent and clean-cut images, young black male hard-core rappers such as Dr. Dre, Tupac Shakur, and Snoop Doggy Dogg continue to face sharp criticism because of their "vulgar" language, their toughened images, and their run-ins with the law. Moreover, young black male rappers are obsessed with the terms and tensions of black manhood, often employing women and gays as rhetorical foils in exploring what they think is authentic masculinity.

Too often, though, a crude reductionism on the part of its critics hampers a truly insightful engagement with gangsta' rap. Like any art form, gangsta' rap allows the creation of a musical persona, an artistic convention honored in opera and even the Tin Pan Alley gangsterism of Frank Sinatra. This convention has been observed in many antecedent black oral traditions, from the long, narrative poems known as toasts to the explicitly vulgar lyrics of Jelly Roll Morton (whose music, by the way, is stored in the Library of Congress) and the ribald and rambunctious reflections of many blues artists.

The wide distribution of recorded music has allowed technological eavesdropping on what formerly were tightly contained communities of vulgar discourse circulated within secular black gatherings. (Note, too, Chaucer's *Canterbury Tales* are strewn with the day's vulgarities; might this mean Snoop Doggy Dogg's "What's My Name" will be read with great reverence, with an eye to imitation, in American classrooms in a couple of centuries?!) These oral traditions, rife with signifying practices, symbolic distortions, and lewd language, must be kept in mind in comprehending and justly criticizing the troubled quest for an enabling black masculinity expressed in much of gangsta' rap.

In this light, the recent attacks on gangsta' rap as fatally misogynistic and deeply sexist by prominent black women like political activist C. Delores Tucker and entertainer Dionne Warwick must be qualified considerably.[22] Gangsta' rap is neither the primary source nor the most nefarious expression of sexism or misogyny, in either society at large or black communities in particular. That honor belongs to cherished branches of our national culture, including the nuclear family, religious communities, and the educational institutions of our society. Black bourgeois civic life, religious communities, and educational institutions have certainly not been immune. These cultural centers that reflect and spread sexist and misogynist mythology—especially the black church, black civil rights organizations, and the black family—much more effectively influence black cultural understandings of gender than does gangsta' rap.

Also, most attacks on gangsta' rap not only continue the widespread demonization of black male youth culture—its alleged out-of-control sexuality, pathological criminality, and sadistic preoccupation with violence—but conceal an attack on black women. Accompanying the wails and whispers of complaint aimed at black males throughout the United States are the detrimental accusations that black males are shaped as they are by black women in single-parent, female-headed households; by welfare queens; or, in the vicious logic that Tucker and Warwick are right to point to, by black mothers who are the bitches and ho's named in many rap lyrics. But Tucker and Warwick often miss the larger point about how their conservative allies in their struggle against gangsta' rap have similarly, but more subtly, demonized black women. (And besides, like most critics, Tucker and Warwick don't mention the homophobia of gangsta' rap; is it because like many mainstream critics, they are not disturbed by sentiments they hold in common with gangsta' rappers?)

The most just manner of criticizing gangsta' rap is by juxtaposing salient features of black culture—such as moral criticism, sage advice, and common-sense admonitions against out-of-bounds behavior—with a ready appreciation of black oral practices like signifying and distorting. By doing this, we can powerfully criticize gangsta' rap for its faults while skillfully avoiding the move of collapsing and corresponding rhetoric and art to reality. Also, we can criticize the conceptions of black masculinity that are prevalent in hip-hop culture without making rappers the scapegoats for all that is seriously wrong with gender in our culture. In the process, we might more clearly see and name the real culprits.

The difficult personal and social conditions of most young black males make Malcolm's rhetoric about the obstacles to true black manhood and the virtues of a strong black masculinity doubly attractive. Indeed, blacks from the very beginning of Malcolm's career have accented his focus on a virile black manhood denied them because of white racism as a primary contribution of his vocation.[23] As Ossie Davis stated in his beautiful eulogy at Malcolm's funeral, "Malcolm was our manhood! This was his meaning to his people."[24] From gang members to preachers, from college students to black intellectuals, Malcolm's focus on black men has made him a critical spokesman for unjustly aggrieved black males plagued by sexual jealousy and social fear.

But if the reemergence of black nationalism and Malcolm's explosive popularity go hand in hand—are duplicate images of response to the continuing plague of an equally rejuvenated racism—then not only their strengths, but also their limitations are mutually revealing. In this regard, two aspects of Malcolm's legacy are striking: the troubling consequences of his focus on the black male predicament, and the ironic uses of black na-

tionalist discourse by a black middle class o.
from nationalism's most desperate constituency—the
ghetto poor.

Malcolm's brand of black nationalism was not only a
fierce attack on white Americans, but a sharp rebuke as well
to black women. Malcolm went to extremes in demonizing
women, saying that the "closest thing to a woman is a
devil." Although he later amended his beliefs, confessing
his regret at "spit[ting] acid at the sisters" and contending
that they should be treated equally, many contemporary
black nationalist advocates have failed to take his changed
position on gender seriously. Malcolm, Patricia Hill Collins
notes, died "before Black feminist politics were articulated
in the 1970s and 1980s," but his

> Black nationalism projects an implicit and highly prob-
> lematic gender analysis. Given today's understanding
> of the gender-specific structures of Black oppression
> . . . his ideas about gender may be interpreted in ways
> detrimental not only to both African-American women
> and men but to policies of Black community develop-
> ment. . . . Malcolm X's treatment of gender reflected
> the widespread belief of his time that, like race, men's
> and women's roles were "natural" and were rooted in
> biological difference.[25]

Like the early Malcolm and other 1960s nationalists,
contemporary black nationalists have defined the quest for

emancipation in largely masculine terms. Such a strategy not only borrows ideological capital from the white patriarchy that has historically demeaned black America, but blunts awareness of how the practice of patriarchy by black men has created another class of victims within black communities.

Further, the strategy of viewing racial oppression exclusively through a male lens distorts the suffering of black women at the hands of white society and blurs the focus on the especially difficult choices that befall black women caught in a sometimes bewildering nexus of kinship groups assembled around race, class, and gender. Reducing black suffering to its lowest common male denominator not only presumes a hierarchy of pain that removes priority from black female struggle, but also trivializes the analysis and actions of black women in the quest for black liberation. Given Malcolm's mature pronouncements, his heirs have reneged on the virtues of his enlightened gender beliefs. It is these heirs, particularly young black filmmakers, whose artistic meditations on black masculinity I will explore in the next chapter.

The cultural renaissance of Malcolm X also embodies the paradoxical nature of black nationalist politics over the past two decades: those most aided by its successes have rarely stuck around to witness the misery of those most hurt by its failures. The truth is that black nationalist rhetoric has helped an expanding black middle class gain increased material comfort, while black nationalism's most desperate constituency, the working class and working poor, continues to toil in the aftermath of nationalism's unrealized political promise.

Ironically, talk of black cultural solidarity and racial loyalty has propelled the careers of intellectuals, cultural artists, and politicians as they seek access to institutions of power and ranks of privilege, even within black communities, as esteemed vox populi. The trouble is they are often cut off from the very people on whose behalf they ostensibly speak, the perks and rewards of success insulating them from the misery of their constituencies.

The greatest irony of contemporary black nationalism may be its use by members of the black middle class—for instance, black intellectuals and artists thoroughly insulated in niches of protection within the academy—to consolidate their class interests *at the expense* of working-class and poor blacks. By refusing to take class seriously—or only half-heartedly as they decry, without irony, the moves of a self-serving black bourgeoisie—many nationalists discard a crucial analytical tool in exploring the causes of black racial and economic suffering. If Malcolm's brand of black nationalism is to have an even more substantive impact on contemporary racial politics, his heirs must relentlessly criticize his limitations while celebrating his heroic embrace of issues, like class and opposing white nationalism, long denied currency in mainstream social thought.

This is not to suggest that nationalism's vaunted alternative, bourgeois liberal integrationism, has enjoyed wide success, either, in bringing the black masses within striking distance of prosperity, or at least to parity with white middle and working classes. Commentators usually gloss over this fact when comparing the legacies of Malcolm X and Martin Luther King, Jr. For the most part, Malcolm and Martin have come to symbolize the parting of paths in black America over the best answer to racial domination. Although Malcolm's strident rhetoric is keyed in by nationalists at the appropriate moments of black disgust with the pace and point of integration, King's conciliatory gestures are evoked by integrationists as the standard of striving for the promised land of racial harmony and economic equity.

In truth, however, King's admirers have also forsaken the bitter lessons of his mature career in deference to the soaring optimism of his dream years.[26] King discerned as early as 1965 that the fundamental problems of black America were economic in nature and that a shift in strategies was necessary for the civil rights movement to become a movement for economic equality. After witnessing wasted human capital in the slums of Watts and Chicago, and after touring the rural wreckage of life in the Mississippi Delta, King became convinced that the only solution to black suffering was to understand it in relation to a capitalist economy that hurt all poor people. He determined that nothing short of a wholesale criticism and overhaul of existing economic arrangements could effectively remedy the predicament of the black poor and working class.

This is a far cry from contemporary black capitalist and business strategies that attempt to address the economic plight of black Americans by creating more black millionaires. Highly paid entertainers and athletes participate in the lucrative culture of consumption by selling their talents to the highest bidder in the marketplace—a legacy, we are often reminded, of King's and the civil rights movement's vision of a just society where social goods are distributed according to merit, not color. King's willingness, toward the end of his life, to question the legitimacy of the present economic order and to challenge the logic of capitalism has been obscured by appeals to his early beliefs about the virtues of integration.

The relative failure of both black nationalist and integrationist strategies to affect large numbers of black Americans beyond the middle and upper classes raises questions about how we can expand Malcolm's and Martin's legacies to address the present crises in black America. What is the answer? I believe the best route for remedy can be found in a new progressive black politics anchored in radical democracy.[27]

Black progressive intellectuals and activists must view class, gender, and sex as crucial components of a complex and insightful explanation of the problems of black America.[28] Such an approach provides a larger range of social and cultural variables from which to choose in depicting the vast array of forces that constrain black economic, political, and social progress. It also acknowledges the radical diversity of experiences within black communities, offering a more realistic possibility of addressing the particular needs of a wide range of blacks: the ghetto poor, gays and lesbians, single black females, working mothers, underemployed black men, and elderly blacks, for instance.

Black progressives must also deepen Malcolm's and Martin's criticisms of capitalism and their leanings toward radical democracy. The prevailing economic policies have contributed to the persistent poverty of the poorest Americans (including great numbers of blacks) and the relative inability of most Americans to reap the real rewards of political democracy and economic empowerment. A radical democratic perspective raises questions about the accountability of the disproportionately wealthy, providing a critical platform for criticizing black capitalist and business strategies that merely replicate unjust economic practices.

A radical democratic perspective—which criticizes capital accumulation and the maximization of profit for the few without regard to its effects on the many, advocates an equitable redistribution of wealth through progressive taxation and the increased financial responsibility of the truly wealthy, and promotes the restructuring of social opportunities for the neediest through public policy and direct political intervention—also encourages the adoption of political and social policies that benefit all Americans, while addressing the specific needs of blacks, such as universal health care.

At present, black Americans are overwhelmingly represented among the 37 million uninsured in our nation. A radical democratic perspective asks why a nation that pays over $820 billion, or 13 percent of the GNP, for the well-insured cannot redistribute its wealth through a progressive tax on the wealthiest 2 percent (and a fair tax on the top 50 percent) to help provide the $50 or $60 billion more needed to provide universal health coverage.[29] By refusing to take class seriously, many black nationalists undermine their ability to completely explain and understand racial and economic suffering.

The quest for black racial and economic justice has been heavily influenced by black religious conceptions of justice, charity, equality, and freedom. During the civil rights movement, King articulated black Christian conceptions of justice through the language of human rights and the political language of civil religion. Likewise, Malcolm X expressed his conceptions of divine retribution for racial injustice, and the religious basis for healthy self-esteem through black Islamic, and later orthodox Islamic, belief that accorded with black secular ideas about racial self-determination and cultural pride. A radical democratic perspective encourages the broad expression of conceptions of justice, equality, and political freedom that are tempered by regard for the widest possible audience of intellectual interlocutors and political participants, including those trained in the rich traditions of black social protest.

Finally, black progressives must make sensible but forceful criticisms of narrow visions of black racial identity, especially after the Clarence Thomas–Anita Hill debacle. That wrenching drama provided a glimpse of the underdeveloped state of gender analysis in most black communities and provoked a serious reconsideration of the politics of racial unity and loyalty.[30] In reflecting on Thomas's nomination to the Supreme Court, black Americans were torn between fidelity to principles of fairness and justice. Many blacks agonized over his qualifications for office and troubled over whether blacks should support one of their own, despite his opposition to many of the legal principles cherished by black communities.

The introduction of Hill's perspective into this already complex calculus ripped open ancient antagonisms between black women and men. The Hill–Thomas affair also affirmed the need for black progressives to pay special attention to the roots of sexism and misogyny in our communities, instead of hitting easy targets like gangsta' rappers. Black progressives must address the pitiful state of gender relations reflected in the lyrics of hip-hop culture, while also addressing the pernicious consequences of the economic misery and social collapse in which they live.

In a public and painful manner, the hearings forced many black Americans to a new awareness of the need to place principles of justice above automatic appeals to race loyalty premised exclusively on skin color. Many Americans, including many blacks, came to a clearer understanding of the idea of the "social construction of racial identity" (which argues that race extends beyond biology to include psychological, cultural, and ideological factors), recognizing that black folk are by no means a homogeneous group. The differences that factors such as geography, sexual preference, gender, and class make in the lives of black Americans are too complex to be captured in a monolithic model of racial unity.[31] Progressive blacks share more ideological and political ground with white progressives such as Barbara Ehrenreich and Stanley Aronowitz, for instance, than they do with conservatives of the ilk of Clarence Thomas, or even Anita Hill.

For black leaders, the political and social significance of this fact should further the building of bridges across the chasm of color in the common embrace of ideals that transcend racial rooting. Progressive blacks must join with progressive Latinas and Latinos, gays and lesbians, feminists, environmental activists, and all others who profess and practice personal and social equality and radical democracy. The relative absence of sustained progressive black political opposition, or even a radical political organization that expresses the views of the working class and working poor, signals a loss of the political courage and nerve in the United States that characterized Malcolm and Martin at their best.[32]

In the end, Malcolm and Martin are in varying degrees captives of their true believers, trapped by literal interpreters who refuse to let them, in Malcolm's words, "turn the corner." The bulk of each man's achievements lay in his willingness to constantly consider and employ new tactics in chiseling the best route to social reconstruction and racial redemption. Their legacy to us is the imagination and energy to pursue the goals of liberation on as wide a scale as the complex nature of our contemporary crises demand and our talents allow.

One segment of black cultural artists in particular— young black filmmakers—have fashioned intriguing and often troubling responses to the issues of thwarted liberation that Malcolm X so boldly raised, especially as they engage the politics of black masculinity and understandings of the ghetto. It is the accomplishments of these artists that I will now explore in seeking to gauge Malcolm X's impact on their lives, most powerfully and painfully in their obsessions with what it means to be a black male in racist white America.

4
IN MALCOLM'S SHADOW: MASCULINITY AND THE GHETTO IN BLACK FILM

> I'm the man you think you are. And if it doesn't take legislation to make you a man and get your rights recognized, don't even talk that legislative talk to me. No, if we're both human beings we'll both do the same thing. And if you want to know what I'll do, figure out what you'll do. I'll do the same thing—only more of it.
>
> Malcolm X, in *Malcolm X Speaks: Selected Speeches and Statements*

The emergence of contemporary black cinema and hip-hop culture marks the wide influence of black popular culture on American life.[1] The work of contemporary black filmmakers embodies the important effort to portray the complexities and particularities of black life. Through the images, symbols, and themes it explores, the new black cinema promises artistic visions of black life that shatter the troubled zone of narrow white interpretations of black culture.

Several recent black films investigate the politics of black masculinity and its relationship to the ghetto culture in which ideals of manhood are nurtured. Debates about masculinity abound in black communities, driven by a need for blacks to understand and address the often tragic circumstances—from high percentages of infant mortality and AIDS infection to staggering rates of imprisonment—that plague black boys and men.[2] Because of the strong link in Malcolm's thought between loyalty to the race and the responsible representation of a disciplined, dignified manhood, he presaged—and continues to influence—the work of contemporary black filmmakers.

Indeed, without the sustained hero worship of Malcolm X, contemporary black cinema, often dubbed New Jack cinema or ghettocentric film, is almost inconceivable. By examining the work of contemporary black filmmakers—the themes they treat, the styles they adopt, the moods they evoke—I seek to gauge Malcolm's ongoing impact on a generation that has driven and seized on his heroic return. In this chapter, I will examine several films as examples of the failure or success in treating the relation between the ghetto and black manhood in powerful and productive ways.[3] In the process, I hope to characterize the manner in which these films engage or distort issues of black female identity.

In his 1991 debut film, *Straight Out of Brooklyn*, director Matty Rich desolately rejects the logic of liberal democracy:

that individuals can act to realize themselves and enhance their freedom through the organs of the community or the state. For the inhabitants of Brooklyn's Red Hook Housing Project, the possibilities of self-realization and freedom are severely reduced by the menacing ubiquity of the ghetto.

The suppressed premise of Rich's film is a rebuke to all pretensions that the ghetto is not a totalizing force, that it is possible to maintain the boundaries between geography and psychic health implied by the expression: live in the ghetto, but don't let the ghetto live in you. It is precisely in showing that the ghetto survives parasitically—that its limits are as small or as large as the bodies it inhabits and destroys—that *Straight Out of Brooklyn* achieves a distinct niche in black film while contributing to black popular culture's avid exploration of black urban (male) identities.

After disappearing from the intellectual gaze of the American academy and being obscured from mainstream cultural view by the successes of nouveau riche yuppies and the newly prominent black middle class, the ghetto has made a comeback at the scene of its defeat. The reinvention of American popular culture by young African-American cultural artists is fueled by paradox: now that they have escaped the fiercely maintained artistic ghetto that once suffocated the greatest achievements of their predecessors, black artists have reinvented the urban ghetto through a nationalist aesthetic strategy that joins racial naturalism and romantic imagination. That the most recent phase of black nationalism is cultural rather than political indicates how successfully mainstream politics has absorbed radical dissent, and betokens the hunger of black youth culture for the intellectual sources of its hypnotic remix of pride and anger.

Mostly anger, and little pride, stirs in the fragmented lives of teenager Dennis Brown (Lawrence Gilliard, Jr.); his younger sister, Carolyn (Barbara Sanon); and their parents, Frankie (Ann D. Sanders) and Ray (George T. Odom). Each of the family members is the prisoner of a personal and ecological misery so great that distinguishing its impact on their lives appears impossible.

The exception to their equally shaded misery is the extraordinarily acute condition of father and son. The black male predicament is first glimpsed in the cinematic chiaroscuro of Ray's descent into a Dantean hell of racial agony so absurd and grotesque that its bleakness is a sadistic comfort, a last stop before absurdity turns to insanity. Ray's gradual decline is suffered stoically by Frankie, a throwback to an earlier era when the black-woman-as-suffering-servant role was thrust on black women by black men, themselves forced to pay obeisance to white society. These same men, when they came home, expected to claim the rewards and privileges of masculinity denied them in the white world. Another model of female identity engaged by black women consisted of an equally punishing (and mythic) black matriarchy that both damned and praised them for an alleged strength of character absent in their feckless male counterparts. Thus the logic of black communities ran: as the black man's fate goes, so goes the fate of the family.

Straight Out of Brooklyn's narrative line ties generously into the fabric of this argument, its dramatic tension drawn from the furious catastrophes that sweep down on its black male characters, the defining center of the film's raw meditation on the angst of emasculation. Ray's frequent beatings of Frankie are rituals of self-destruction, her brutally bloodied countenance a sign of his will to redefine the shape of his agony by redefining the shape of her face.

Ray's suffering-as-emasculation is further sealed by his denial of desire for white women during a Lear-like verbal jousting with an imaginary white man, a deus ex machina produced by his search for an explanation of his suffering, and a dramatic ploy by Rich that ascribes black suffering to the omnipotent white bogeyman. And Dennis's soliloquies about his quest for money to reverse his family's collapse in the presence of his girlfriend, Shirley (Reana E. Drummond), underscores a deeper need to redeem black masculinity by displaying his virility, his desire to provide for his family allied disastrously with his gratuitous desires to "get paid."

A different tack is pursued, of course, in John Singleton's 1991 debut, *Boyz N the Hood*. Singleton's neorealist representation of the black working-class ghetto neighborhood provides a fluid background to his literate script, which condenses and recasts the debates on black manhood that have filled the black American independent press for the past decade.[4] Avoiding the heavy-handed approach of racial didacticism, Singleton instead traces the outline of the morality play in recognizable black cultural form. All the while, he keeps his film focused on The Message: black men must raise black boys if they are to become healthy black men. Thus Tre (Cuba Gooding, Jr.); his father, Furious (Laurence Fishburne); Ricky (Morris Chestnut); and Doughboy (Ice Cube), the four black males whose lives form the fabric of Singleton's narrative quilt, are the films's interpretive center. Reva (Angela Bassett), Brenda Baker (Tyra Ferrell), and Brandi (Nia Long), the mothers of Tre and of Ricky and Doughboy, and Tre's girlfriend, respectively, occupy the film's distant periphery.

As in most cultural responses to black male crisis, Singleton's film is an attempt to answer Marvin Gaye's plea to save the babies. He focuses his lens especially on the male baby that he and many others believe has been thrown out with the bathwater to float down the river, like Doughboy and one out of four black men, into the waiting hands of the prison warden.

Singleton's moral premise, like so many assertions of black male suffering, rests dangerously on the shoulders of a tragic racial triage: black male salvation at the expense of black female suffering, black male autonomy at the cost of black female subordination, black male dignity at the cost of black female infirmity. In jarring fashion, Singleton's film reveals the unintended but deadly alliance between black cultural nationalists and the cultured despisers of black women. His thinly veiled swipe at black women fuses easily with the arguments of conservative cultural commentators who bash poor and working-class black women as promiscuous welfare queens. Furious's brilliant presence as a redemptive and unswerving North Star and Brenda's uncertain orbit as a dim satellite are the telling contrast in Singleton's cinematic world.

Singleton's moral premise would seem outdated—the warmed-up leftovers of black macho posturing painfully evident in strains of 1960s black nationalism—were it not for its countless updates in black youth culture. Such sentiments are also expressed in rap lyrics, for instance, that denounce white racism while glorifying black males' sexual and material mastery of black women. Of course, the quest for black manhood is everywhere apparent in black culture—note its evocation as well in the upper climes of respectable bourgeois life as the implicit backdrop to Clarence Thomas's claim of betrayal by Anita Hill, his charge communicated in the racial code of his undertone: another *sister* pulling a *brother* down. But it is with the reemergence of the ghetto in popular culture and its prominence in a resurgent black nationalist cultural politics that lionizes Malcolm X that for better and worse the images of black masculinity find an intellectual home.

This circumstance is especially true of black film and rap music. The politics of cultural nationalism has re-emerged precisely as the escalation of racist hostility has been redirected toward poor black people. Given the crisis of black bourgeois political leadership and a greater crisis of black liberal social imagination about the roots of black suffering, black nationalist politics becomes for many blacks the logical means of remedy and resistance. This explains in part the renewed popularity of Malcolm X, whose uncompromising focus on nationalist themes of unity and authentic blackness help secure his heroic niche in black youth culture. Viewed in this way, black film and rap music are the embodiment of a black populist aesthetic that prevents authentic blackness from being fatally diluted.

Rap music has grown from its origins in New York's inner city over a decade ago as a musical outlet for creative cultural energies and as a way to contest the invisibility of the ghetto in mainstream American society.[5] Rap remythologized New York's status as the spiritual center of black America, boldly asserting appropriation and collage as its primary artistic strategies. Rap developed as a relatively independent artistic expression of black male rebellion against a black bourgeois worldview, tapping instead into the cultural virtues and vices of the so-called underclass. Male rap artists romanticize the ghetto as the fertile root of cultural identity and racial authenticity, asserting that knowledge of ghetto styles and sensibilities provides a Rorschach test of legitimate masculinity.[6]

The styles and sensibilities encouraged in the hip-hop aesthetic have found expression in many recent black films. Mario Van Peebles's 1991 directoral debut, *New Jack City*, for instance, boils with the fusion of ghetto attitude and style that expresses a substantive politics of culture among young black males. As in *Boyz N the Hood* with Ice Cube (Doughboy) and *Juice* with Tupac Shakur (Bishop), *New Jack City* appeals directly to the ironic surplus of hip-hop culture by drawing on a main character, rapper Ice-T, to convey the film's thinly supplied and poorly argued moral message: crime doesn't pay.

Thus Ice-T's "new jack cop" is an inside joke, a hip-hop reconfiguration of the tales of terror Ice-T explodes on wax as a lethal pimp, dope dealer, and bitch hater. The adoption of the interchangeable persona of the criminal and "the law" in hip-hop culture is taken to its extreme with Ice-T's character. Although he appears as a cop in *New Jack City*, Ice-T on the soundtrack as a rapper detailing his exploits as a "gangsta'" blurs the moral distinctions between cops and robbers, criminalizing the redemptive intent of his film character (even more so retroactively in light of the subsequent controversy over his hit "Cop Killer," recorded with his speed metal band).

Van Peebles's cinematic choices in *New Jack City* reflect a mode of exaggerated cultural representation that characterizes many ghetto films of old. His ghetto is a sinister and languid dungeon of human filth and greed drawn equally from cartoon and camp. Its sheer artifice is meant to convey the inhuman consequences of living in this enclave of civic horror, but its overdrawn dimensions reveal a cinematic pedigree traced more easily to 1970s blaxploitation flicks than to neorealist portrayals of the ghetto in recent black films.

As a black gangster film, *New Jack City* reveals the Cagneyization of black ghetto life, the inexorable force of woman bashing and partner killing sweeping the hidden icon of the people to a visible position larger than life. Thus criminal Nino Brown (Wesley Snipes) reigns because he tests the limits of the American Dream, a Horatio Alger in blackface who pulls himself up by forging consensus among his peers that his life is a ghetto jeremiad, a strident protest against the unjust material limits imposed on black males. As Nino Brown intones with full awareness of the irony of his criminal vocation: "You got to rob to get rich in the Reagan era."

But it is the state of black male love that is the story's unnarrated plot, its twisted pursuit ironically and tragically trumped by boys seeking to become men by killing one another. Thus when a crying Nino clasps his teary-eyed closest friend and partner in crime, Gee-Money, on the top of the apartment building that provides the mise-en-scène for the proverbial ode to an empire destroyed by the fatal winds of undisciplined ambition, he avows his love even as he fills Gee-Money's belly with steel as recompense for disloyalty. It is the tough love of the gang in action, the logic of vengeance passing as justice in gang love's fulfillment of its unstated obligations.

The mostly black and Latino gang, of course, has also recaptured the focus of American social theory and journalism in the past decade. Urban sociologists such as New York's Terry Williams in *Cocaine Kids* and Los Angeles's Mike Davis in *City of Quartz* have written insightfully about the economic and social conditions that have led to the emergence of contemporary black and Latino gang culture.[7] And model turned journalist Leon Bing has interviewed Los Angeles gang members who speak eloquently about their own lives in words as moving for their emotional directness as their honesty about the need for affection and comfort that drives them together.[8] In *Straight Out of Brooklyn* and in Ernest Dickerson's *Juice*, the theme of black male love expressed in the ghetto gang looms large.

In *Straight Out of Brooklyn*, Rich presents a loosely associated group of three black male teens, Dennis, Kevin (Mark Malone), and Larry (played by Rich), who are frustrated by poverty and the stifling of opportunity that lack of money signifies. In *Juice*, the crushing consequences of capital's absence are more skillfully explored through the

117

interactions between the characters (its damning effects as subtly evoked in the threads of anger, surrender, and regret weaved into the moral texture of the film's dialogue as they are dramatically revealed in the teens' action in the streets); in *Straight Out of Brooklyn*, money's power is more crudely symbolized in the material and sexual icons that dominate the landscape of desire expressed by Dennis and his friends: big cars, more money, and mo' ho's.

The lifelessness of the ghetto is represented in the very textu(r)al construction through which *Straight Out of Brooklyn* comes to us. Although it's in color, the film seems eerily black and white, its crude terms of representation established by its harsh video quality and its horizontal dialogue. Of course, the film's unavoidable amateur rawness is its premise of poignancy: after all, this is art imitating life, the vision of Matty Rich, a nineteen-year-old Brooklyn youth with little financial aid committing his life to film. This is the closest derivation in film of the guerrilla methods of hip-hop music culture, the sheer projection of will—onto an artistic canvas composed of the rudimentary elements of one's life—in the guise of vision and message.

In *Straight Out of Brooklyn*, the trio of teens is not a roving, menacing crew engaging in the business of selling crack rock and duplicating capitalism's excesses on their native terrain. Rather, they are forced by desperation to momentary relief of their conditions by robbing a dope dealer, an impulse that is routinized in the crack gang, where rituals of gunplay and death feed on the lives of opponents out to seize their turf in the harrowing geopolitics of the drug economy.

The anomie produced by everyday acts of surrender to despair, and the spiraling violence of his father, Ray, force Dennis from his family to affectionate camaraderie with Larry and Kevin, and with Shirley. All other hints of family are absent, except Larry's barber uncle, who unwittingly provides the ill-named getaway car for their even more ill-fated heist. But the vacuum at home for Dennis is made more obvious by Ray's attempt to preserve the disappearing remnants of a "traditional" family: he angrily reminds Dennis after he misses dinner that his empty plate on the table symbolizes his membership in the family. But Rich shatters this icon into shards of ironic judgment on the nuclear family, as Ray breaks the dishes and beats Frankie each time he becomes drunk.

Dennis's only relief is Shirley and his crew. When Shirley disappoints him by refusing to buy into his logic about escape from the ghetto by robbery, he turns to his crew, who, in the final analysis, leave Dennis to his own wits when they agree that they have stolen too much cash ("killing money," Kevin says) from the local dope dealer, an act whose consequences roll back on Dennis in bitter irony when the heist leads to his father's death. The film's inescapably dismal conclusion is that black men cannot depend on one another, nor can they depend on their own dreams to find a way past mutual destruction.

In *Juice*, the crew is more tightly organized than in *Straight Out of Brooklyn*, though their activity, like that of the teens from Red Hook, is not regularized primarily for economic profit. Their salient function is as a surrogate family, their substitute kinship formed around their protection of one another from rival gangs, and the camaraderie and social support their association brings. But trouble penetrates the tightly webbed group when the gangster ambitions of Bishop threaten their equanimity. Of all the crew—leader Raheem, a teenage father; GQ, a DJ with ambitions to refine his craft; and Steel, a likable youth who is most notably "the follower"—Bishop is the one who wants to take them to the next level, to make them like the hard-core gangsters he watches on television.

Viewing Cagney's famed ending in *White Heat*, and a news bulletin announcing the death of an acquaintance as he attempted armed robbery, Bishop rises to proclaim Cagney's and their friend's oneness, lauding their commendable bravado by taking their fate into their own hands and remaking the world on their own violent terms. Dickerson's aim is transparent: to highlight the link between violence and criminality fostered in the collective American imagination by television, a medium whose images compete with the Constitution and the Declaration of Independence for supplying the unifying fictions of national citizenship and identity. Television is also the daily and exclusive occupation of Bishop's listless father, a reminder that its influence unfolds from its dulling effects in one generation to its creation of lethal desires in the next, twin strategies of destruction when applied in the black male ghetto.

Like the teens in *Straight Out of Brooklyn*, *Juice's* crew must endure the fatal consequences of their failed attempt at getting paid and living large, two oft-repeated mantras of material abundance in the lexicon of hip-hop culture. After Bishop's determination to seize immortality leads him to kill the owner of the store his crew robs, the terms of his Faustian bargain are more clearly revealed when he then kills Raheem, destroying all claims of brotherhood with a malicious act of machismo, succeeding to Raheem's throne through murder.

Dickerson, who has colorfully photographed most of Spike Lee's films, uses darker hues in *Juice* but nowhere near the drained colored canvas on which *Straight Out of Brooklyn* is drawn. Dickerson's moral strategy is to elaborate to its fatal ends the contradictory logic of the gang as a family unit, a faulty premise as far as he is concerned because it overlooks the gang's lack of moral constraints and the destructive consequences it breeds. Dickerson's aesthetic and directorial strategy is to move the cameras with the action from the observer's frame of reference, borrowing a few pages from Lee's book without mimicking Lee's panache for decentering the observer through unusual angles and the fast pace of editing. Like Rich in *Straight Out of Brooklyn*, Dickerson wants the impact of his message to hit home, but his methods are not as harsh as Rich's. Instead, he draws us into his moral worldview with an invitation to view the spectacle of black male loss of love by degrees and effects.

The ghetto working-class family in *Juice* is much more visible and vital than the one in *Straight Out of Brooklyn*. Mothers and fathers wake their children in the morning for breakfast and make certain they take their books to school. The notion of extended family and "fictive kin" is even given a nice twist when GQ fetches a gun from one of his mother's old friends, a small-time neighborhood supplier.[9] And Dickerson subtly draws attention to the contrasts between the aesthetic and moral worldviews of the generations, and the thriving of an earlier era's values among the younger generation, at the dinner at Raheem's family's house after Raheem's funeral.

As snatches of gospel music float gently through the house, GQ and Steel pay their respects to Raheem's family. But when Bishop arrives, the rupture between generational values forces to the surface the choice each of the remaining three crew must make. GQ and Steel are offended at Bishop's effrontery, his mean-spirited hypocrisy leading him to violate Raheem's memory with this latest act of machismo and pride. For them, the choice is clear. The religious values signified in the quiet gospel music seem no longer foreign, providing a gentle counterpoint to the hip-hop aesthetic of violent metaphors used in the service of greater self-expression.

Instead, the gospel music and the world of black respectability that it symbolizes carry over into GQ's and Steel's grieving acknowledgment of the bonds between them and their departed friend, a sure sign that religious consciousness survives in them no matter how distant the teens appear to be from its redemptive effects. Bishop's desecration of Raheem's memory and family signify the depth of Bishop's moral failure, embodying the reckless abandon to which his acts of violence have given cruel expression. Unlike the black teens in *Straight Out of Brooklyn*'s ghetto, the black males can depend on one another, but only after being encouraged to acknowledge their debts to the moral vision of an older culture, and only after discovering the limits of their freedom in destructive alliance with one another.

In sharp contrast to *Juice*—which portrays the pernicious effects of generational decline and narrates the carnage of fratricide from within the arc of traditional black morality—the Hughes brothers' brilliant, disturbing 1992 debut, *Menace II Society*, unblinkingly unveils the absurdity and terror that cloak young black male ghetto life. Their terse, lean script—complemented by the cast's surprising economy of emotional expression, given the genre's tendency to trumpet more than whisper—counterpoints the unwieldy realities the film brutually reveals: postindustrial urban collapse, the ravaging personal and social effects of underground drug economies, the sheer violence of everyday life in the ghetto, and the destruction of black male life.

From the opening scene, where "Old Dog" (Larenz Tate) makes his childhood friend (Tyrin Turner) an unwitting partner in crime by murdering the Korean owner of the store they visit, to the film's finish, where Turner's character is gunned down as he attempts to escape Los Angeles and enjoy a more promising life in Atlanta with his girlfriend and her son, *Menace II Society* exposes the contradictory impulses of black male life that fuel its hope even as it ensures its destruction. *Menace II Society*, even more than *Juice* (or the Oliver Stone–produced *South Central*), registers the raw realities of black ghetto life in the message that black men are both one another's greatest allies and most lethal enemies. Turner's narration throughout the film—bringing coherence to a world, and his own life, fragmented by the forces of violence and retribution that mark the rhythm of urban existence—reveals an ironic hopefulness and even a muted moral passion that redeem young black life *on its own terms.*

The contemporary debate within black culture about black film and its enabling or destructive representations of black males and black females started with the meteoric rise of Spike Lee. With Lee's groundbreaking *She's Gotta Have It*, young black men laid hold of a cultural and artistic form—

the Hollywood film—from which they had with rare exception been previously barred. In gaining access to film as directors, they began to seize interpretive and representational authority from what they deemed ignorant or insensitive cultural elites whose cinematic portrayals of blacks were contorted or hackneyed, the ridiculously bloated or painfully shriveled disfigurements of black life seen from outside black culture. Lee's arrival promised a new day beyond stereotype.

What we get with Lee, however, is Jungian archetype, frozen snapshots of moods in the black male psyche photographed to brilliant effect by Ernest Dickerson. Lee's mission to represent the various streams of black life denied cinematic outlets has led him to resolve the complexity of black culture into rigid categories of being that hollow his characterss' fierce and contradictory rumblings toward authentic humanity.[10] And after *She's Gotta Have It*, black women became context clues for the exploration of black male rituals of social bonding (*School Daze*), the negotiation of black male styles of social resistance (*Do the Right Thing*), the expansion and pursuit of black male artistic ambitions (*Mo' Better Blues*), or the resolution of black male penis politics (*Jungle Fever*).

Lee's cinematic representations of black male life occasioned sound and fury over his most important project to date: his film biography of Malcolm X. As a reigning icon of black popular culture, Malcolm's autobiography is the Ur-text of contemporary black nationalism. Because his legacy is claimed by fiercely competing groups within black America, Lee's film was a hard sell to some factions. More important, since Malcolm's complex legacy has only recently been opened to critical review and wider cultural scrutiny, his admirers and detractors have rushed forward to have their say once again.

To many, however, Malcolm is black manhood squared, the unadulterated truth of white racism ever on his tongue, the unity of black people ever on his agenda, the pain of black ghetto dwellers ever on his mind. Thus the films that I have discussed, which also represent the visual arm of black nationalism's revival, bear in many ways the burden of Malcolm X's presence in every frame, his philosophy touching every aspect of the issues they deal in: drugs, morality, religion, ghetto life, and, especially, the conditions of being a black man. For many, as for his eulogist Ossie Davis, Malcolm embodied the primordial, quintessential Real Man.

But as with the films of Dickerson, Lee, Rich, Singleton, and Van Peebles, this focus on black masculinity spells real trouble for black women. Perhaps only when more major-studio black films begin to be directed by black women will the repertoire of identities that black women command be adequately represented on the large screen. Powerful gestures toward black female–centered film exist in the work of Julie Dash in *Daughters of the Dust* and especially in Leslie Harris's *Just Another Girl on the IRT*. But until the cultural and economic barriers that prevent the flourishing of films by black women are removed, such works threaten to become exceptions to the rule of black male film.

In the meantime, black male directors remain preoccupied, even trapped, by the quest for an enabling conception of male identity. Such an enterprise will continue to be hampered until black male filmmakers explore masculinity's relationship to black women, promoting ideas of black masculinity that dissolve its links to the worst traits of Malcolm's lethal sexism. (John Singleton's 1993 *Poetic Justice*, however, failed dismally; its attempt to explore the life of a young black female [Janet Jackson] was fatally frustrated as the film's center turned quickly, and unapologetically, to the struggles of her male companion [Tupac Shakur]). Gestures of Malcolm's new attitude survive in the short hereafter Malcolm enjoyed on his escape from Elijah Muhummad's ideological straitjacket. Malcolm's split from the Nation of Islam demanded a powerful act of will and self-reinvention, an unsparing commitment to self-critical reflection, a trait that led him to reject his former hostility to (black) women.

But this is not the aspect of Malcolm most remarked on by his contemporary imitators who champion his return to prominence. Is this the Malcolm who emerges in Spike Lee's cinematic portrait of the slain leader? This question, of course, entails many others. What are the costs of presenting Malcolm's complexity on screen? Can Lee break the mold of severely limited female agency that characterizes his work and the work of his black film contemporaries up to this point? What happens to Malcolm when his life is treated by a cultural nationalist who is also a bourgeois black artist? I turn my attention now to Lee's film biography of Malcolm, the most important cultural representation of the black cultural hero yet created, in search of answers.

5
SPIKE'S MALCOLM

> When you teach a man to hate his lips, the lips that
> God gave him, the shape of his nose that God gave him,
> the texture of the hair that God gave him, the color of
> the skin that God gave him, you've committed the
> worst crime that a race of people can commit. And this
> is the crime you've committed. . . . This is how you im-
> prisoned us. Not just bringing us over here and making
> us slaves. But the image that you created of our moth-
> erland and the image that you created of our people
> on that continent was a trap, was a prison, was a chain,
> was the worst form of slavery that has ever been in-
> vented by a so-called civilized race and a civilized na-
> tion since the beginning of the world.
>
> Malcolm X, in *Malcolm X: The Last Speeches*

Malcolm X's intellectual legacy and his representation in
popular culture are often, not surprisingly, at odds with
each other. Although the stated point of analytical investigations of Malcolm's life is to probe the roots of his thought
and action with critical sophistication and intellectual rigor,
artistic treatments of Malcolm's career encourage a greater,
freer use of the imagination. Although art may occasionally
dispense with "fact" (since, at its best, art reveals cultural
biases that shape radically opposed interpretations of
events), it has an obligation to tell, if not *the* truth, then *its*
truth.

MALCOLM X IN CONTEMPORARY SOCIETY

In Malcolm's case in particular, making choices about how to portray him on film are indivisible from the long, bitter struggle to bring his life to the screen at all.[1] As David Bradley argues, Hollywood "didn't keep firing writers from the 'X' project because the scripts were wrong. They kept firing writers because the *story* was wrong."[2] If Malcolm's story, then, was too controversial to bring to the big lights, too prickly for bourgeois formulas about racial problems and their smooth, painless removal, then what kind of Malcolm worth anything could possibly survive Hollywood's pulverizing machinery? And of the Malcolms being advanced by conflicting cultural constituencies for a starring role—including Malcolm as symbol of racial hatred and violence, Malcolm as black nationalist, Malcolm as newly minted American cultural icon, Malcolm as revolutionary internationalist, Malcolm as weak integrationist, Malcolm as reborn humanist—which one would ultimately make the cut?

These questions barely graze the interpretive and cultural complexities that Spike Lee confronted as he set out to make history and *his* film on Malcolm X. From the start, Lee was embroiled in controversy as he sought to seize control of the project from white director Norman Jewison. whom Lee believed categorically incapable of telling the story of not just any black man, but the quintessential Angry Black Man and, by extension, the urban black American. Lee played the politics of racial privilege with cunning, but barely before his success had settled in, he in turn came under attack for his anticipated mistreatment of Malcolm.

Even before filming began, writer and social critic Amiri Baraka drew blood in a war of words with Lee, asserting that Lee's poor history of representing black men meant that he would savage the memory of Malcolm X—a memory, by the way, to which Baraka presumed to have special access—loading onto Malcolm's historical frame Lee's own bourgeois distortions. This battle between the two diminutive firebrands, ironic for its poignant portrayal of the only logical outcome of the politics of more-black-nationalist-than-thou—a game Lee himself has played with relish on occasion—was but a foretaste of the warfare of interpretation to come because of Lee's portrait of Malcolm.

Besides these considerations, Lee's shrewd and, at times, crass commercialization of Malcolm's memory—plus his grandstanding public-relations stunts meant to make his film a guaranteed draw (for instance, telling children to skip school to see his film on opening day)—raised serious questions about his integrity in doing the film. Lee's merchandising of Malcolm memorabilia led many to conclude that he was hustling Malcolm's history to his own financial advantage. Plus Lee's methods of promotion appeared to some a bourgeois exploitation of black nationalist politics severed from a real commitment to the working-class and poor constituency Malcolm loved. And ironically, Lee, who has often been perceived in the white media as a hotheaded filmmaker and racial firebrand, became, in the eyes of many, the vehicle for the mass production and dilution of Malcolm X as an acceptable, easily packaged, even chic commodity that Lee sold in his film and in his 40 Acres and a Mule Shops.

In light of these realities, and the inherent difficulties of cinematically representing a man whose life has been reconstructed by webs of myth and romance, however, Lee's *Malcolm X* is still an often impressive, occasionally stunning achievement. It is a richly textured and subtly nuanced evocation of the life and times of a supremely American paradox: a onetime racial particularist whose fame has been shaped to display his belated, if confusing, universal appeal.

Lee's Malcolm is inevitably a creation of Lee's own oversized ambitions. He has reframed the racial themes of his earlier work around the shadow figure at its spiritual core.[3] In *School Daze*, Lee ridiculed the petty but pernicious politics of skin color that abound within black culture, an echo of Malcolm's warnings against the ubiquitous threat of black self-hate. In *Do the Right Thing*, Lee dashed the easy sentimentalism that often prevails in integration-minded talk about racial progress and harmony, a favorite rhetorical trump in Malcolm's shuffling and dealing of the racial deck. And in *Jungle Fever*, Lee explored the fatal conflicts that can ensnare interracial romance, which in his view and in the view of the early Malcolm is a chasm of pathology.

Spike's Malcolm

In *Malcolm X*, Lee's racial ruminations, which have often spun out of control, have found their artistic apotheosis. The last time Lee integrated Malcolm into one of his films, Malcolm's words about violence in aid of black liberation served as a textual coda to *Do the Right Thing*, his sentiments set in black and white, much like the image Lee conjured of Malcolm in that context. But Lee's understanding of Malcolm has matured since Malcolm was used to supply a stylized signature to Lee's own racial reflections.

The genre of *Malcolm X*—the epic—and the film's real-life subject impose historical limits, aesthetic constraints, and artistic conventions that work wonders for Lee's treatment of the complexities of race. The field of fire sparked before filming began by his battles with the writer Baraka and others over the "correct" representation of Malcolm made Lee's job virtually impossible. Satisfying the varying constituencies that have a stake in shaping the memory of Malcolm is no small task, and it is the sort that few directors have faced. The directors of comparable epic films—David Lean (*Lawrence of Arabia*) and Sir Richard Attenborough (*Gandhi*)—confronted nothing like the scale of attack that Lee endured in the battle over Malcolm's legacy.

The three hours and twenty-one minutes Lee takes to explore Malcolm's life are divided between the three major stages in his career: as street hustler and criminal; as devotee of Elijah Muhammad and preacher par excellence of black nationalism; and as an independent black leader who formed two organizations, the Muslim Mosque and the Organization of Afro-American Unity, to reflect his changed religious and political views after his departure from the Nation of Islam and his pilgrimage to Mecca. Lee seems to rush through the last stage with dizzying and distorting speed, leaving largely untouched Malcolm's visit to Africa and the substantial broadening of his ideological perspective. Lee's pace may be unintentional, but it is nevertheless effective in dramatizing the almost desperate improvisation that Malcolm displayed. He lived less than a year after his break with the Nation of Islam, and no matter how much we want to fill in the blanks, a definitive account of his latter days is hard to come by.

The tripartite division of the life follows faithfully the lineaments of Malcolm's various emergences and conversions as detailed in his autobiography (as told to Alex Haley), *The Autobiography of Malcolm X*.[4] That text itself has been criticized for avoiding or distorting certain facts. Indeed, the autobiography is as much a testament to Haley's ingenuity in shaping the manuscript as it is a record of Malcolm's own attempt to tell his story. The profound personal, intellectual, and ideological changes Malcolm was undergoing near the end of his life led him to order the events of his life to support a mythology of metamorphosis and transformation that bore fruit in spiritual wisdom. But that document bears deep traces as well of Malcolm's attempt to fend against the inevitable vulnerabilities revealed in the process of recalling and reconstructing one's life. In simple terms, this means that Malcolm's claim that he was expelled from West Junior High School in Lansing, Michigan, for instance, is inaccurate; he slid through the seventh grade there in 1939. In a more profound manner, however, Malcolm never mentions his meeting with the Ku Klux Klan in 1961 to see if that group, which like the Nation of Islam espoused racial separatism, could help Elijah Muhammad and his followers obtain land to implement their beliefs.[5]

As with most autobiographies, Malcolm's recollections were an effort to impose order on the fragments of his experience. The story of his escape from functional illiteracy, his exodus from mental and social slavery, and his conversion to true belief—only to have that belief betrayed by the father figure of his faith—is a narrative whose philosophical pedigree draws on Augustine, Booker T. Washington, Frederick Douglass, and Sigmund Freud. To the extent that Lee embellishes the historical account, he is being faithful in a way to the spirit of self–re-creation that Malcolm evidenced in his colorful telling of his own life.

Oscar-winning actor Denzel Washington invests the early Malcolm, then known as Malcolm Little and eventually as Detroit Red, with a canny and charismatic mix of steely determination and unpolished naïveté. He plays perfectly Malcolm's entree into the black hustling world at the awkward age of fifteen. The mix of awe and aspiration is captured on Washington's face when he is spotted and wooed by Sophia (Kate Vernon), a white woman at the ballroom where he and his partner Shorty (played by Lee) are jitterbugging. In *Jungle Fever*, Lee cluttered his examination of interracial love with diverting, confusing stories about drugs and adultery. Here Malcolm's experience places a cinematic loop around Lee's treatment. The moral of the story is the same as in Lee's earlier coverage: interracial love is lethal and self-destructive. But the historical context and racial rationale of that moral is given a denser treatment. Lee's version is drawn from Malcolm's early and middle rhetoric, not from his later declarations to James Farmer and others that interracial love is a personal, not a political, choice.

Lee evokes the criminal phase of Malcolm's career with a vibrant and dream-time palette of colors that suggests the hustling life's attraction to people of color in the 1940s and 1950s. All too often, cinematic treatments of black street life are reduced to an appendage of chic white goings-on (as in Francis Ford Coppola's *The Cotton Club*) or a cartoonish colored approximation of a parallel white street buffoonery (as in Eddie Murphy's *Harlem Nights*). With Lee, we feel the pulse and passion of the streets through a hodgepodge of crafty and stylized characters who possess intelligence and dignity. Later in the film, however, Lee addresses the brutish and seedy underside of that life, which gets canned and canonized as black cultural pathology in the lazy eyes of social theory in journalistic dress, and gets viewed as the harmful and insidious symptom of white racist neglect in the black puritanism of the Nation of Islam that Malcolm preached.

West Indian Archie, played with smooth and seductive equanimity by Delroy Lindo, is the embodiment, in both the autobiography and Lee's film, of the misled ingenuity that betrays the citizen of the street when his or her life is severed from a black religious mooring. Although he takes the young Malcolm under his wing, it is he who, after a dispute over money in his numbers racket, eventually forces Malcolm to flee Harlem and return to Boston, the scene of his earliest hustling, before his fateful turn in prison. West Indian Archie is both father and foil to Malcolm, and thus a foreshadowing of the treachery he will confront in Elijah Muhammad.

Here and throughout his film, Lee conflates characters: West Indian Archie (mentioned in the autobiography) and his cronies stand in for Sammy the Pimp and others in the autobiography who befriended Malcolm and showed him the ropes of hustling. In the prison sequence, Lee produces a fictional character named Baines (Albert Hall), who accomplishes the work of both the disciplined prisoner Bimbi in the autobiography (who told Malcolm that he "had some brains" and should use them) and his brother Reginald, who along with his other brother, Philbert, had become a member of the Nation of Islam. Reginald advised Malcolm that if he didn't "eat any more pork" or "smoke any more cigarettes,'' he would show Malcolm how to get out of prison.

Lee's tactic finds precedence in Malcolm himself, who conceded that Shorty was a composite of characters. And as in Malcolm's case, perhaps, Lee's strategy allows him to avoid dealing with some painful truths. By making Baines the source of Malcolm's conversion, Lee doesn't have to unravel the messy ironies involved when Malcolm observed the enforced shunning of Reginald, the very brother who had introduced him to the faith. And by making Baines the traitor to Malcolm because of his (and other Nation ministers') resentment of Malcolm's prominence in the white media, Lee avoids laying the blame for the jealousy at the feet of its likely source, Elijah Muhammad, whose quirky resonances are deftly presented in the charming and gnomish bearing of Al Freeman, Jr. Lee escapes as well explaining the betrayal and renunciation of Malcolm by two of his brothers in the Nation after his assassination.

Lee's choices make sound cinematic sense for the most part, especially in his treatment of Malcolm's slow awakening from an unconscious worship of the white world. Lee takes his time, allowing us to watch the unraveling of layer upon layer of resistance to the truth that Elijah Muhammad brought: that the white man is a ''devil,'' that black people are the true masters of the universe, that white culture has throughout the world left death and destruction in its wake.

This was strong brew for a black male barely out of his

teens whose "conked" hair style reflected his esteem for the white world. "It look white, don't it?" he asks after getting his hair processed for the first time, seeking the approval of other black men who had endured the painful process of relaxing their stiffened manes.

Lee is especially effective in portraying the profound spirituality that marked Malcolm's mature years and that was the source of an eerie poise in the midst of social upheaval and personal crisis. The markers of black spirituality have been dominated by the Christian cosmos; the themes, images, and ideas of black spiritual life are usually evoked by gospel choirs enthralled in joyous praise or a passionate preacher engaged in ecstatic proclamation. Never before in American cinema has an alternative black spirituality been so intelligently presented. One montage of Malcolm's rhetorical ripostes and verbal volleys extends, incredibly, for several minutes. And throughout Lee's treatment of Malcolm's Nation of Islam stage, his words, thoughts, and ideas and those of the Nation are vigorously presented. This is no small achievement in our anti-intellectual environment, which punishes the constituency that has made Malcolm its hero: black teens and young adults.

Lee portrays Malcolm's extraordinary self-possession when, without words, he waves away the followers who have collected to make certain that justice will be rendered by white New York police after a beating of one of the "brothers." The police captain both acknowledges and laments Malcolm's quiet authority, saying, "That's too much power for one man to have." Malcolm's balance would eventually collapse under the threat to his life posed by Nation loyalists who resented Malcolm's rebuff of Elijah Muhammad and who hatefully hounded him during his last few months, inducing in Malcolm a psychic vertigo that Lee only barely captures.

By contrast, and in keeping with the hagiographical tendencies of all epic films, Lee presents Malcolm near the end as harried but hushed, a man of saintly moral attainment. Lee's intent to portray Malcolm as having it all together on the inside while his world crumbles around him not only is romantic, but does a disservice finally to the greater truth that Malcolm continued to work even in the midst of the palpable premonition of his quickly approaching death.

The murder scene is one of the most brilliantly staged film accounts of the emotional pitch and pandemonium surrounding an assassination. As is true throughout the film, Lee's choice of period music is haunting and effective. As Malcolm glides toward death at Harlem's Audubon Ballroom in his sleek Oldsmobile 98, the sweetly agonizing verse of "A Change Is Gonna Come" (penned and sung by former gospel great Sam Cooke, another black genius killed in his prime) captures Malcolm's impossible predicament. Cooke's pathos-brimmed melisma reminds us that though it's been "too hard living," he's "afraid to die."

Although Lee's Malcolm is more subdued, even softer, than many had wished—possessed less by strident rage than by hard-won wisdom—he survives the Hollywood machinery and remains a provocative, valuable figure. Still, Lee's Malcolm speaks rhetoric that is a far cry from the volatile, incendiary talk that the police and government feared would be spewed by Malcolm's character and that would incite riots in theaters on opening night. That fear, as with Lee's earlier *Do the Right Thing*, reflects a tragic lack of awareness about the dynamics of racial rage and the suitable targets of its expression. Such racial paranoia prevented many filmgoers from viewing the film in its theatrical release.

Interesting as well is Lee's portrayal of Malcolm's finely nuanced relationship with his wife, Betty Shabazz, whose mellow thunder and independent temperament are sketched with revealing concentration by Angela Bassett. Shabazz was alternately supportive and sternly self-willed (she left Malcolm after the birth of each of their first three children). But Shabazz's affectionately sparring relationship with Malcolm, especially over gender roles, is only slightly acknowledged in the film.

There are other absences. Chief among them is Louis Farrakhan, former calypso singer, Malcolm's onetime associate turned enemy, and the current leader of the Nation of Islam. The bad blood between Malcolm and Farrakhan and the Nation of Islam continues to this day, despite Farrakhan's moderation of his sentiments expressed in the

1964 statement that "a man such as Malcolm deserves to die." Absent, too, is the figure of Muhammad Ali, who was led into the Nation by Malcolm and was a huge attraction to young black men. The two had a falling-out over Malcolm's departure from Elijah Muhammad's ranks. A few years later, though, Ali himself would be straitjacketed by the Nation, leading to his eventual passage into the precincts of orthodox Islam.

One might also quibble about the unnecessary didacticism of the film after the assassination. In this part, staged in classrooms in the United States and South Africa, children repeat, "I am Malcolm X," to indicate their inheritance of the fallen leader's legacy. This move is Lee's attempt to solve cinematically a perplexing condition: how to get black youth to identify with the redemptive message of Malcolm's racial edification. It comes off as needlessly contrived and facile, but it reveals just how difficult the task of reaching black youth really is. Still, Lee's failed attempt at least forces us to concede how our most desperate attempts to address the problems of black youth, either through law and order or by appealing to an ethical norm in a golden past of black tradition, have likewise failed.

The appearance of Nelson Mandela, before his ascent to the presidency of South Africa, is at once riveting and revealing. In an ironically poignant coda, Mandela's presence reinforces for our eyes the difficult lot of *living* heroes, his well-worn visage registering complexities of fate that in figures like King and Malcolm are swept away by the sacred wash of early martyrdom. At the end of Mandela's speech about Malcolm and black freedom, it is not Mandela's voice but Malcolm's that utters the widely quoted and more widely misunderstood phrase "by any means necessary." One senses at that moment, albeit ever so slightly, the loss of heroic authority that marks our era and that sends millions back to the words of a dead man for hope.

Like *The Autobiography of Malcolm X*, Lee's work avoids uncomfortable questions about Malcolm's alleged homosexual alliances during his hustling days, the ambiguous events surrounding the burning of his Nation-owned home (and allegations that Malcolm himself set the fire), doubts about whether Malcolm's father died at the hands of revenge-minded white racists (a scenario Lee reproduces), and Malcolm's skillful manipulation of white media fascinated by his rhetorical excesses.

Nevertheless, Lee has rendered the life of an American original in terms that are both poignant and insightful. Above all, in taking the risk of defining and interpreting a figure entwined in racial and cultural controversy, he has sent us back into our own memories, or to books and documentaries, in search of the truth for ourselves. And he has done more than that. He has set the nation talking about a figure whose life deserves to be discussed, whose achievements deserve critical scrutiny, and whose career merits the widest possible exposure. Many great films have achieved considerably less than that.

Lee's film has contributed significantly to the renewed heroism of Malcolm X among black and other Americans. But the enormous buildup to his film has also, ironically, contained and capped the interest in the leader it has inspired. Now the real work of intellectual and political recovery and reconstruction of Malcolm's legacy must begin.

What are the most powerful, liberating uses to which Malcolm's legacy can be put? What is Malcolm's meaning to the black males who have invested heavily in his heroic return, especially as their fortunes continue to decline? And how will the progressive vision of race encouraged by Malcolm's mature philosophy fare in the age of Clinton? I will attempt to answer these questions in the final chapter.

6
USING MALCOLM: HEROISM, COLLECTIVE MEMORY, AND THE CRISIS OF BLACK MALES

> It's not wrong to expect justice. It's not wrong to expect freedom. It's not wrong to expect equality. If Patrick Henry and all of the Founding Fathers of this country were willing to lay down their lives to get what you are enjoying today, then it's time for you to realize that a large, ever-increasing number of Black people in this country are willing to die for what we know is due us by birth.
>
> Malcolm X, in *Malcolm X: The Last Speeches*

Malcolm X's heroism not only is linked to the resurgence of black nationalism and a revived racism to which it forcefully responds, but draws as well from a grand tradition of black heroism that dates back to slavery. A significant feature of historic black heroism is the stimulation and preservation of cultural achievement through collective memory.[1] Thus the achievements of heroes and movements from the black past were ceaselessly evoked in black communities in oral and written form as an inspiration to continued thought and action in the same vein. The logic of such strategies hinged on the belief that if other blacks in the past could perform heroic activities, and often under brutal circumstances that defied adequate description, then blacks in succeeding historical eras could surmount obstacles to racial achievement.

Another closely related function of collective memory was its use as "an instrument of survival."[2] Through the stories black folk have always told one another about a history filled with accomplishment and failure—tales about incredible feats performed against inhuman odds as well as bitter accounts of justice denied, of opportunities missed, and of dreams and lives cut short prematurely—they have managed to negotiate the treacherous terrain of American life with their lives intact.

The celebration of Malcolm's memory, then, has cultural and racial precedent. I want to examine briefly the roots of an African-American heroism that illumines Malcolm's legacy, while exploring varieties of collective memory in suggesting how Malcolm's memory may be useful now. I will also examine the progressive vision of race inspired by Malcolm's latter-day humanist philosophy. Perhaps the greatest use of Malcolm's memory today can be in dissolving the links that connect the tragic triangle of self-hatred, violence, and racism that plagues the constituency

most invested in Malcolm's cultural return: young black
males. Because the collective morale of young black males
is threatened, I will suggest helpful ways to think about
their vexing problems.

In African-American culture, heroic traditions have
usually developed in response to forces of oppression, especially white racism in various forms: chattel slavery, black
codes, Jim Crow, separate-but-equal laws, lynching, cas-
tration, and the like. During slavery, heroes were seen as
figures who resisted racial dominance through slave insur-
rections, plantation rebellions, work slowdowns, or running
away.[3] Leaders like Denmark Vesey, Gabriel Prosser, Harriet
Tubman, and Nat Turner acquired mythic stature as heroes
because they defied white rule during slavery.

After slavery, when African-American society faced
enormous obstacles in reshaping a culture that had been
deliberately undermined by the forces of white racism and
vulgar capitalism, heroic action consisted of the continued
battle against racist oppression in various forms. Most notably, black heroism was viewed in autobiographical stories
of escape from slavery, the rehabilitation of African-
American culture through political action, and the remaking of the moral life of African-American communities in
religious affiliation and spiritual devotion.[4] Figures like
Frederick Douglass, Henry Turner, Sojourner Truth, and
Henry Highland Garnett became heroes during Reconstruction.

From slavery until the present, African-American heroes have been instrumental in preserving the collective
memory of black culture against the detrimental consequences of racial amnesia while fighting racism in American
public culture.[5] The collective memory of black Americans
countered the racial amnesia represented in the selective
memory of the recent American past in white America. As
Michael Kammen has pointed out, selective memory expresses the desire for reconciliation—through strategies
of depoliticization and amnesia—by dominant traditions
that obscure or distort the collective memory of minority
traditions.[6]

In discussing the heroic use of collective memory by
African-Americans, Kammen describes how selective memory "kept African-Americans outside the mainstream of
retrospective consciousness," leading to blacks' perpetuat-
ing their own heroic "traditions and memories." From "the
mid-1880s onward, therefore, African-Americans largely
celebrated their heroes and pursued their own historic occasions alone."[7] African-Americans' "collective memory of
slavery remained vivid," and "what they chose to emphasize by means of traditional activities each year was the
memory of gaining freedom."[8]

Frederick Douglass in large measure carved out his heroic niche in African-American culture by advocating a tradition of collective memory that fought racial amnesia:

It is not well to forget the past. Memory was given to man for some wise purpose. The past is . . . the mirror in which we may discern the dim outlines of the future. . . . Well the nation may forget, it may shut its eyes to the past, and frown upon any who may do otherwise, but the colored people of this country are bound to keep the past in lively memory till justice shall be done them.[9]

It is the quest for social justice in a racist society, along with the preservation of collective memory, that has forged a powerful connection between earlier expressions and contemporary varieties of black heroism. Malcolm X fits easily into this tradition. Both progressive and conservative views of collective memory may be useful in viewing Malcolm's life.

In discussing twentieth-century studies on collective memory, Barry Schwartz makes a distinction between two views. The first view, a progressivist or constructionist one, "sees the past as a social construction shaped by the concerns and needs of the present."[10] This approach draws on the work of George Herbert Mead and Maurice Halbwachs in showing how conceptions of the past are drawn from contemporary problems and how collective memory reconstructs the past by adapting the images of past beliefs to present historical needs.[11]

The second perspective on collective memory, a conservative one, "is distorted in a different direction: It is the past that shapes our understanding of the present rather than the other way around."[12] This perspective draws on the work of Emile Durkheim and Edward Shils in contending that commemoration rites reproduce the past, while offering an understanding of a stable tradition that transmits a common heritage.[13] As Schwartz maintains, the conservative view "draws attention to continuities in our perceptions of the past and to the way these perceptions are maintained in the face of social change."[14]

Both views have relevance for African-American uses of collective memory in preserving heroic images of Malcolm and in combating paralyzing forms of political and racial amnesia. The contention that the past is constructed from present historical needs contains a powerful—if partial—insight about the function of contemporary struggles in not merely preserving, but also re-creating, memories of Malcolm. This view accents the agency of contemporary participants in the heroic tradition of response to racism that he so imaginatively represented.

This view also actively includes the intellectual contributions of contemporary participants in reshaping a tradition of heroic response to racism given to them by Malcolm. It confirms, too, the flexibility of traditions of social protest, encouraging the rejection of literal interpretations of heroic figures that make narrow notions of loyalty to their ideas a prerequisite for participation. This view provides welcome relief from heroic celebrations of Malcolm that turn on strict and selective interpretations of his social and historical meaning. A constructionist approach to the collective memory about Malcolm stresses the ongoing evolution of understanding about his career that acknowledges the many uses to which his memory may be put in reaching the goals he expressed.

Finally, this understanding encourages the expansion of social criticism and moral vision that Malcolm represented, inviting criticism of aspects of his legacy that undermine the needs of contemporary participants. For example, Malcolm's sexism is a significant blight on his achievements. Principled opposition to his gender blindness actually encourages the observation of broader principles of fairness and justice that Malcolm cherished.

The more conservative approach to collective memory, though, ensures an attention to historical detail that guards against romantic fictions and unrestrained myths that so easily attach to Malcolm's career. This conservative approach emphasizes the historical character of Malcolm's career, linking present observations about his heroism to interpretations of his rhetoric, practice, and behavior in accounting for his enduring racial significance.

This perspective also encourages a more lucid explanation of the complex positions Malcolm adopted throughout his career and an exploration of how his radical transformations of thought reflected a self-critical posture.

The Malcolm that has often been lost in hero worship is the Malcolm who could be critical of himself as well as the society that treated black people with fundamental disrespect. This is the most promising dimension of Malcolm's legacy that we can extend: a willingness to see the errors of our ways, to acknowledge that without sometimes severe self-criticism black folk will never achieve the true measure of our intended greatness as a people.

The conservative view of collective memory carries with it a rebuke to all who believe that they have the *definitive* view of Malcolm X without critically engaging his life and thought. Those who spare Malcolm from criticism do his legacy the most harm. For his best ideas and most powerful insights to flourish in our present historical context, they must be subjected to thorough examination. Only then can we understand and measure his true greatness, acknowledging his accomplishments and failures as we assess his place in our national history.

Among the most helpful ways that Malcolm's memory may be used in our contemporary moment is to develop a powerful defense of radical democracy and a sharp criticism of race and racism in the age of Clinton. Malcolm's antiracist speech anticipated the sort of keen, no-nonsense analysis and action we must undertake, especially when our nation's political condition seems to favor, on its surface, the interests and aspirations of most African-Americans. But as Malcolm so clearly understood, it is just such a "favorable" political climate that may encourage the worst offenses against black interests, because those figures in violation of black progress shield themselves from attack under cover of an often unmerited black loyalty. As Malcolm might muse, a political wolf in sheep's clothing often does more harm to black folk than an explicit enemy.

President Clinton's policies and actions so far indicate that he may be just the sort of political figure Malcolm often warned us against. Clinton's public positions on race encourage clever but often unprincipled manipulations, even distortions, of racial rhetoric in our national life. A brief look at recent racial history will help illuminate the hopes of racial progress that Bill Clinton has come to embody and, I think, annul in his time in office.

For the past twelve years, fateful changes in American culture have sapped our nation's ability to speak about race with informed passion. The collapse of the will to undo the legacy of past racial injustice with immediate intervention, through either governmental sponsorship or the beneficent public action of the private sector, has left a gaping hole in the patchwork of remedies that at our most hopeful moments we imagined could remove the bruising inequalities that continue to haunt us.

Also, the fierce rivalry among previously despised or ignored groups for a visible stake in the politics of public attention has masked the source of their anxieties: that too often, social goods are parceled out as so many concessions to demands by the strongest group in a system of reward held hostage by zero-sum thinking. African-Americans, women, Latinos and Latinas, and Asian-Americans are often pitted against one another in a battle for scarce resources—a sour arrangement indeed, for they aren't the source of one another's primary pains. In this light, all the noise about "special interest groups" seems a disingenuous denial of the factors that led minorities to adopt competition as their stock-in-trade to begin with.

Moreover, the thinly veiled contempt for racial minorities during the Reagan and Bush administrations unleashed a racist backlash, the worse effects of which had been held in check by the gains of the civil rights movement and the altered social landscape it brought into existence. For those who point out that even that arrangement was dishonest (that it simply shifted racism underground, concealing the persistence of bigotry that conforms the American character to its ugly, irrational image), a word of caution is in order. To paraphrase Ernest Becker, the American character may be a lie, but it's a *vital* lie. Some forms of restraint that protect the possibility of rational dialogue and humane behavior must be retained as we work through the occasionally deadly consequences of reordering our unjust racial practices.

To this end, the election of Bill Clinton promised a breath of fresh air, and in some ways, his presidency has been refreshing. The hoopla surrounding his ascendancy marked a return to the rituals of public participation in power largely absent since the gilded mythology of John Kennedy's Camelot, and more narrowly glimpsed in the cowboy captivity of Ronald Reagan's reign. Clinton's charm with the media, his crafting of a persona as the American everyperson who invites his constituency to become partners in reshaping American democracy around the common good, and his revival of a vocabulary of national service have all combined to make his appeal larger and more humane than that of his Republican predecessors.

Clinton's cabinet appointments reflected his stab at a new direction. Undeniably, Clinton was plagued early on by his asleep-at-the wheel handling of the attorney general "nanny-gate" affair, which both betrayed his ignorance of the average citizen's perspective and documented his insensitivity to child-care issues. Overall, however, Clinton pulled in racial minorities and women to make his official advisers "look more like America" than before. But his bristling at pressure to appoint more women, as he responded that he wouldn't "count beans," revealed that he is more closely allied with George Bush's principles of gender and race relations than was initially believed. Clinton's unprincipled about-face on the Haitians coercively sequestered at Guantanamo Bay and his vicious repatriation of Haitians seeking asylum from political tyranny (a policy on which he finally relented only after Randall Robinson's hunger strike and protest from the Congressional Black Caucus) only reinforce this suspicion.

The real danger of race in the age of Clinton is a cautionary tale about "friendly fire," the unintended wounds inflicted by alleged friends, not the deliberate assaults of enemies. (No one knows this more painfully than Clinton's friend Lani Guinier, whom Clinton proposed to head the Civil Rights Division at the Department of Justice. Clinton's abandoning of Guinier after she was unfairly dubbed a "quota queen" by the *Wall Street Journal*, and his refusal to permit her a fair hearing before the Senate after the tide of public opinion turned against her, only reinforced the perception that Clinton was quite willing to sacrifice loyalty for popularity.)

During his campaign, Clinton expanded the influence of the conservative Democratic Leadership Council, a group composed of disgruntled neoliberals formed after the collapse of traditional liberalism within the Democratic party. Signs of this conservatism, especially in regard to race, flashed during the presidential campaign when Clinton employed the code phrase "winning back the suburbs." By using this phrase, Clinton implicitly distanced himself from the pain and perspectives of the working class and the ghetto poor. The gesture not only smacked of hubris—the premise was that he didn't need poor blacks and Latinos and Latinas, and that middle-class minority support was already sewn up—but further endangered the racial goodwill that many citizens, especially progressives, had expected from Clinton.

Such hopes of racial goodwill were dealt a further blow with Clinton's exploitative treatment of Sister Souljah, aping the rancid public-relations maneuvers associated with the late Lee Atwater's symbolic manipulation of white suburban angst in the infamous Willie Horton affair. Clinton's cynical and opportunistic response to rapper Sister Souljah's comments that blacks should harm white folk during the urban rebellion in Los Angeles revealed the flawed character of much liberal thought about race in America. Perhaps Clinton was seeking to generate moral revenue by investing in Dan Quayle's school of shallow ethical analysis or looking to bolster his sagging campaign, but the timing and venue of opportunity for Clinton's remarks suggested something tragically awry.

Why did Clinton wait so long before responding to Sister Souljah's comments? On the face of it, his camp's contention that swift reaction by Clinton would have been viewed as gratuitous seemed to wash. But it is more likely that neither Clinton nor his handlers had any idea of Sister Souljah's existence before she made her observations. Her sole importance to Clinton derived from Sister Souljah's symbolic worth in his quest to make a highly visible, if unprincipled, moral gesture. Moreover, by making his remarks at the Rainbow Conference, where Sister Souljah had appeared the previous day, Clinton distanced himself ideologically from Jesse Jackson and rang the register of race suspicion while appearing to practice racial fairness.

But his gain was the American citizenry's loss. Clinton blew a prime opportunity to become a public moralist, to move beyond the treacherous insinuations and finger-pointing that abound in discussions of race and to teach us something genuinely useful about the ethical consequences of racial desperation. Sister Souljah's statements certainly warranted careful critical commentary. But Clinton might have as easily acknowledged the extreme difficulty of adequately responding to social forces that have made Los Angeles a powerful symbol of the postindustrial urban crises that fueled the riots and evoked the rapper's sharp observations. By drawing attention to Souljah, Clinton chose an easy target. He also avoided the more challenging task of addressing the futility embodied in Souljah's sentiments and in the cultural expression of many young blacks, especially hip-hop artists.

What Clinton failed to grasp—a trait he shares with many American intellectuals and leaders—is that, like Malcolm, rappers channel black rage and defiant rhetoric at the conditions that make life hell for urban residents. At its best, rap entails a refusal of silent complicity in the social and political destruction of black life by offering sometimes rude rebukes to the white and black powers-that-be. Of course, rap is sometimes intoxicated with its own candor and rightness of cause, leading to rhetorical excesses that are sometimes more desperate passion than hateful harangue.

Had Clinton played to his announced strengths of sharp social and political analysis, he could have challenged Sister Souljah's understanding of the political utility of violence by linking a discussion of the Los Angeles rebellion with previous incarnations in Detroit and Watts. This turn of conversation might have led to an insightful discussion of the loss of political will and imagination around remedying the problems generated by race and class. And where better to launch such a project than at the Rainbow Conference. Standing on Jesse Jackson's political terrain and going toe-to-toe in a much needed debate about these issues?

Instead, Clinton shrank moral ambiguity and racial desperation to simplistic terms. He searched through the fortuitous arrangements of a lately lackluster schedule to seize a golden, if gratuitous, opportunity to shine. In so doing, Clinton betrayed his desire to broaden liberal political debates about race beyond hackneyed phrases, contemptuous posturing, and stifling opportunism. That such debates are sorely needed is demonstrated by the character of most cultural criticism expressed in the aftermath of Clinton's attack on Sister Souljah. Praising Clinton for his righteous rhetorical ripostes to Souljah's sentiments, lauding his jettisoning of Jackson from the moderate ship of liberalism that Clinton sails, or condemning Jackson for his condemnations of Clinton, most commentary was moralistic and narrow. The real moral tragedy is that neoliberal race theorists and practitioners have underplayed or misdiagnosed the urban blight, social hopelessness, and thinly veiled anger that give rise to raw and sometimes misdirected statements like those made by Sister Souljah.

Young black ghetto residents, a major constituency of rap music, have remained invisible to the Bill Clintons of the world until they serve useful political purposes that have nothing redemptive to say about their painful predicament. By playing to the greatest fears of disaffected, dropout white Democratic voters at the expense of loyal black Democrats (and only after the primaries were over), Clinton displayed the ugliest sort of political opportunism.

When she appeared on the "Phil Donahue Show" in the winter of 1991, Sister Souljah revealed that she had grown up on welfare in the Bronx, escaped poverty, studied in Spain, and won a scholarship to Rutgers. Her ridiculous statement about harming white people—after all, most people who died in the riots were people of color—was a departure from her severe but articulate defense of black nationalism. Of course, Bill Clinton didn't know this, because he used her for his small purposes and not our larger learning.

Despite these signs of a lapsed faculty for principled debate about the future of race, there is lingering hope that Clinton can recover moral ground and begin to speak and think about race in complex and productive ways. Equally important, there is still hope that the new era he aspires to embody will encourage the elaboration of radical democratic tendencies within our culture. Such activity can help lift the veil of fear and ignorance about racial difference, a veil that reinforces the structural political and economic inequities already eroding the lives of many minorities.

For now the end of the Reagan–Bush era, more than the beginning of the age of Clinton, contains the seeds of hope for radical democrats and other progressives and antiracists. Because we are losing a clear target to aim for—one of the virtues, after all, of outright opponents is that they encourage outright opposition—radical democrats must become even more vigilant in clarifying the terms of antiracist struggle in our culture. Inspired by the example of the mature Malcolm X, and the radical democratic views he began to express near the end of his life, such a project can find a broad base of support.

One of the major forms such struggle should take is continued opposition to the pernicious stereotyping of black women as the symbol bearers for the afflictions of the welfare system. Conservatives like Charles Murray contend that if we could somehow improve poor black women's initiative, their will to upward mobility, we could solve the problem of a congenital welfare syndrome. Most conservative analyses of welfare dependency and initiative (to which Clinton seems inclined) are notoriously one-sided, neglecting the structural factors that prevent black women from flourishing.

For instance, initiative is often dependent on the amount of reward one receives for it. One's motivation to continually seek employment will not be high when there is little prospect of finding it. In this scenario, initiative expresses the relation between expectation and reward. What kinds of jobs are available? What kinds of education or training does the employment seeker have? To what kinds of education or training has she or he had access? What are the structural changes in the economy that affect the viability of the kind of work the person does? What are the chances for education or retraining? What is the person's relation to the informal network of information that often influences employment chances? These are simply a few of the questions that must be pressed in assessing the level of initiative present and in understanding how one can relate initiative to a larger range of factors.

A radical democratic rethinking of such questions, buttressed by investigations of the social causes behind the fragile place of poor black women in the economy; an understanding of the sexist employment force, in which women continue to earn only 70 percent of what men make for comparable work; and an explanation of the dominance of the service industry over manufacturing, which has eroded the wage base of poor black women, compromising their ability to support their families, might help place initiative in a more illumined framework. Further, comprehending the effects on women of the casualization of labor and honestly acknowledging the disincentives to initiative contained in regulations that bar women from supplementing their welfare incomes with work would chasten those who call for simpleminded workfare solutions that tie welfare benefits to employment.

The radical democratic antiracist struggle must continue to oppose racist violence, manifested most recently in the Rodney King beating in Los Angeles. While the riot that followed the acquittal of the police officers who savagely assaulted King is a complex phenomenon, the conditions that provoked that social rebellion remain buried in poor communities across the United States. For the past decade, rap artists—who as informal ethnographers of black youth culture translate the inarticulate suffering of poor black masses into articulate anger—have warned of the genocidal consequences of ghetto life for poor blacks. Their narratives, though plagued by vicious forms of misogyny and homophobia that merit strong criticism, communicate the absurdity and desperation, the chronic hopelessness, that festers inside the postindustrial urban center. Police brutality is a recurring theme of rap narratives, generated by young black males victimized by the unchecked exercise of state repression. Radical democrats must take the lead in criticizing the actions and rhetoric of prominent figures who help shape a national climate where racist violence, particularly police brutality, seems a plausible or unpunishable action.

The radical democratic antiracist struggle should, in Malcolm's spirit, oppose all forms of oppression while constantly forging links with other progressive peoples and organizations. Religion, for example, continues to play a significant role in the lives of Latinos and Latinas and of African-Americans, and it remains a major route of entry into a common politics of opposition to racism within their communities. Given the erosion of moral community across our nation, religion continues to provide moral strength and insight for millions of people through narratives of personal transcendence, ethical responsibility, and spiritual nurture. Especially within minority communities, where issues of meaning and morality are often fused with politics in prophetic religious practices, religion can provide a means of personal stability and social criticism. Radical democrats must continue to overcome antireligious sentiment if we expect to connect with many African-Americans, and Latinas and Latinos, for whom it is relevant to talk of God while speaking of human community.

Particularly within African-American communities, the fight against racism has centered in black religion. With their noble articulation of the norm of fundamental human equality and their strong insistence on black worth, black religionists (Christian and Muslim) are suspicious of secular ideologies that deny the validity of religious experience. Conversely, the strength of radical democratic philosophy and practice has been its unblinking description of the ills associated with forms of thought and political practice shaped by unjust forces, some of which were maintained by religious belief.

These mutual suspicions may be put to good use as black religionists and radical democrats join forces in the reconstitution of the civic order and the reconstruction of political practice. Radical democratic thought can provide a rich vocabulary of social criticism to engage the varied forms of social inequality that prevail in black communities across America. And black religion can offer a needed emphasis on the moral dimensions of political practice and social criticism. Black religionists can insist on anchoring such practice and criticism in a perspective that values human life and asserts the priority of meaning as a fundamental goal of human life.

Given Bill Clinton's identification with the politics of meaning, and his advocacy of the virtues of placing discussions about the common good at the center of American political discourse, radical democrats can make headway by pushing him to broaden his understanding of the problems of race. Radical democrats must urge Clinton to live up to his inaugural-ceremony rhetoric about springtime in the United States. Otherwise, the calamitous consequences of racial domination and violence will make it the long winter of our nation's discontent, especially for a population hit hard by these forces—black men. Malcolm's memory can help us understand and combat the precarious predicament of young black males in America, even if by only forcing our nation to acknowledge its role in their condition.

Urban America is living through an epidemic of violence that has targeted and viciously transformed black male life.[15] With chilling redundancy, black men are dying at the hands of other black men. The mutual harming of black males is a thematic mainstay of the contemporary black films I discuss in Chapter 3. Such films portray the cruel consequences of urban collapse on black male life. The situation for black men, especially juvenile and young adult males, is now so fatally encrusted in chronic hopelessness that terms usually reserved for large-scale social catastrophes—terms like "genocide" and "endangered species"—are now applied to a wide variety of black males with troubling regularity.[16]

Many cultural critics, especially conservative commentators, have concluded that black male violence is the exclusive result of pathological cultural tendencies working themselves out with self-destructive fury. On this view, black male aggression is part of a larger black cultural malaise manifest in welfare dependence, criminal lifestyles, gang activity, and other morally impaired behavior associated with an ominously expanding "underclass." And even when more reasonable critics, especially politically liberal figures, weigh in on the causes and consequences of black male violence, their analyses often skid dangerously close to reductionist cultural arguments that blame the victims of violence for its existence.

Because the situation of black males has become so formidably complex, the horizon of clarity often recedes behind vigorous yet confusing attempts to understand and explain their predicament. Can Malcolm X's example and memory in any way help black men past mutual destruction and the threat of social annihilation? How should we proceed in thinking about these highly charged, complex issues?

In combating the crisis of black males, we must first comprehend the staggering array of difficulties that hound and hurry them from the cradle to the grave. Malcolm was keen on scrupulously documenting the truth of black life, a trait that led him to combine common-sense observation and critical investigation in detailing the plight of African-Americans. In this vein, the extent of social injuries to black male life is indexed in the virtually mind-numbing statistics whose mere recital is the most powerful testimony to a hydra-headed crisis.

Black males are more likely than any other group to be spontaneously aborted. Of all babies, black males have the lowest birth weights. Black males have the highest infant mortality rates. Black males have the greatest chance of dying before they reach age 20. Although they are only 6 percent of the U.S. population, blacks make up half the male prisoners in local, state, and federal jails. Thirty-two percent of black men have incomes below the poverty level. Fifty percent of black men under 21 are unemployed. But it doesn't end here.

Between 1980 and 1985, the life expectancy for white males increased from 63 to 74.6 years; for black males, only from 59 to 65. Between 1973 and 1986, the real earnings of black males between the ages of 18 and 29 fell 31 percent, as the percentage of young black males in the work force plummeted 20 percent. Suicide is the third-leading cause of death among young black men. And as noted earlier, black-on-black homicide is the leading cause of death for black males between the ages of 15 and 34, as young black males have a 1-in-21 lifetime chance of being killed. This is not new; in 1987 alone, more young black men were killed within the United States in a single year than had been killed abroad in the entire nine years of the Vietnam War. This deadly pattern of problems, which accumulates without apparent abatement and taxes black male mortality beyond expected limits—makes it difficult to view the black male condition as the product primarily of black cultural failure.

Next, we should place black male suffering in a historical framework that illumines how black males, far earlier than their recent troubles suggest, have been culturally fashioned as a "problem" category. From the plantation to the postindustrial city, black males have been seen as brutishly behaved, morally flawed, uniquely ugly, and fatally oversexed. The creation of negative black male images through the organs of popular culture—especially in theological tracts, novels, and, more recently, film and television—simply reinforced stereotypes of black males as undisciplined social pariahs, citizens of a corrupt subculture of crime, or imbeciles. Add to that the influence of scholarly portrayals of black males, particularly those contained in ethnographic studies that have both aided and undermined the cultural status of black men, and one gets a hint of the forces challenging a balanced interpretation of their condition.

Finally, we must pay attention to the structural factors that spawn black male suffering. As Malcolm preached a year before his death, "Unemployment and poverty have forced many of our people into [a] life of crime."[17] The shift of the labor base of black males from high-wage, low-skill jobs to scarcer service employment; the expanding technical monopoly of information services; the part-timing of American labor (leaving workers without employee benefits); and the wrenching of the U.S. economy by crises in global capitalism all bode ill for black males.[18] These changes, coupled with cycles of persistent poverty, the gentrification of inner-city living space, the juvenilization of crime, and the demoralization of poor blacks through cultural stereotypes about widespread loss of initiative, only compound the anguish of an already untenable situation for black males.

I am not suggesting that we can reduce the black male crisis to its economic or social determinants. Nor do I contend that black males are without responsibility for elements of their condition. Indeed, the example of Malcolm's black moral puritanism—which promoted self-reliance, rigorous self-discipline, a strong work ethic, and law-abiding behavior—is a rebuke to black males who profess to follow his example while shirking personal and moral responsibilities to their families and communities.

I am simply arguing that the debate about black males must become much more complex and sophisticated, that its participants must be more honest in unearthing the roots of black male agony. It is much easier to damn black males for being irresponsible, immoral, or even criminal than to own up to how American cultural traditions and economic practices have contributed to their plight. Malcolm believed that

> the real criminal is the white man who poses as a liberal—the political hypocrite. And it is these legal crooks, posing as our friends, [who are] forcing us into a life of crime and then using us to spread the white man's evil vices among own people. Our people are scientifically maneuvered by the white man into a life of poverty. You are not poor accidentally. He maneuvers you into poverty. . . . There is nothing about your condition here in America that is an accident.[19]

Although Malcolm's conspiracy theory of history ascribes too much responsibility to individual whites, his words underscore an understanding that American society bears significant responsibility for the plight of black males.

This is perhaps most tragically true of the spiritual fatigue and psychic trauma occasioned by racism, and the black male self-hate that it engenders, most viciously expressed in black-on-black homicide, but also insidiously present in less conspicuous gestures of mutual black male contempt. After all, black males have not been immune to the destructive influence of negative cultural messages about themselves, fatally absorbing surface and subtle reminders that their lives are perishable and expendable, less valuable than white lives, and not as useful as those of famous figures like Michael Jordan and Bill Cosby. Malcolm poignantly described the self-hatred that sits at the heart of black-on-black crime:

> We hated our heads, we hated the shape of our nose . . . we hated the color of our skin, hated the blood of Africa that was in our veins. And in hating our features and our skin and our blood, why we had to end up hating ourselves. . . . It made us feel inferior; it made us feel inadequate; made us helpless.[20]

Neither have young black males resisted the seductions of violence; the addictive character of aggression is symptomatic of American popular culture from hockey to Hollywood. It is this combination of violence, racism, self-hatred, and economic desperation that makes black male life vulnerable to confused and often unfair criticism. But if we are to solve the problem of violent black males, we must solve their problems. To paraphrase the great Catholic social prophet Dorothy Day, we must work toward a world in which it is *possible* for black males to behave decently.

Malcolm's memory may yet help save an entire generation of black males buffetted by brutal forms of racial and class antagonism from outside black culture, and beseiged by internal demons and temptations, from drug addiction and violence directed against one another, from within. His wise, salvific offer of comfort to black males—that they are worthy of the highest measures of respect and love—came wrapped in poignant demands of self-discipline and racial uplift. And his heroic example of relentlessly questioning his own unjust thoughts and deeds, leading him to reject narrow racialism and blind gender scapegoating, remains the truest and most meaningful monument to black manhood. Perhaps more than when he first spoke and lived them, Malcolm's words and deeds carry profound import for black males at the dawning of our first full century of American freedom.

Malcolm X's words and deeds can also spur us on to great efforts: they can move us to build on his most valuable ideas even as we are encouraged to transcend his failures and weaknesses. We can confirm his true significance as a prophetic orator and fearless spokesman by acting to enflesh the ideals of humane community and progressive political action he didn't live long enough to see become a reality. By this measure, the greatest achievements of the heroic tradition Malcolm X participated in remain in the future.

AFTERWORD
TURNING THE CORNER

> The only person who can organize the man in the
> street is the one who is unacceptable to the white com-
> munity. They don't trust the other kind. They don't
> know who controls his actions. . . . The greatest mis-
> take of the movement has been trying to organize a
> sleeping people around specific goals. You have to
> wake the people up . . . to their humanity, to their
> own worth, and to their heritage. The biggest differ-
> ence between the parallel oppression of the Jew and
> the Negro is that the Jew never lost his pride in being
> a Jew. He never ceased to be a man. He knew he had
> made a significant contribution to the world, and his
> sense of his own value gave him the courage to fight
> back. It enabled him to act and think independently,
> unlike our people and our leaders.
>
> Malcolm X, in *Malcolm X Speaks:*
> *Selected Speeches and Statements*

Since Malcolm's death in 1965, black Americans have wit-
nessed the arrival of pretenders and wannabees to his
throne of rage. There have been many lesser incarnations
of Malcolm's prophetic spirit and rhetorical passion, men
and women who believed that all that was in Malcolm's bag
of tricks was loud speech and hateful harangue. (Khalid
Abdul Muhammad's ad hominem attacks on black leaders
and Jews is only the most recent example.) Although Mal-

175

colm's withering words would sometimes transport vicious verbal assassinations of other black leaders—and though he could be stubbornly, willfully blind to the truth of a situation that stared him straight in the face—he learned, finally, to make his rage work for the best interests of black folk. That included learning to work with people—like Martin Luther King, Jr., and other leaders of a civil rights movement that he grew to respect for its masked radicalism—with whom he didn't always agree, in fact to whom he'd formerly been vehemently opposed.

Malcolm also came to believe that real leadership was empowering people to lead themselves, to eventually do without the mortal suffering that he had endured at the hands of charismatic but corrupt leadership. Malcolm's push near the end of his life was for people to learn and grow as much as they could in the struggle to free mind and body from the poisonous persistence of racism and blind ethnic loyalty, as well as economic and class slavery. He apologized for his former mistakes, took his lumps for things he'd done wrong in the past, and tried to move on, even though, as he lamented, many devotees (and enemies) wouldn't allow him to "turn the corner." For Malcolm's sake, and for the sake of our survival, black folk must turn the corner.

But what does turning the corner mean for us now? It means that we must turn away from the easy scapegoating of other minorities and ethnic groups in assigning blame for our pain. The problems between blacks and Jews, for instance, are much ballyhooed and bemoaned. Of course, with countless pressing problems facing black communities, we must ask why the media has given so much attention to black–Jewish relations.

In large measure, the media has exploited conflicts between blacks and Jews by imbuing them with an almost surreal intensity and by helping to construct black anti-Semitism as a much more pervasive and virulent phenomenon than empirical research can support. The media has fanned the flames of alleged black discontent with Jews by irresponsible reporting that fails to place relations between the two groups in historical and political perspective. While the fractures of spirit and face suffered by aggrieved parties on both sides are significant, the deeper truth is that these tensions are part of a broader conflict between African-American communities and other groups. Because the black–Jewish compact is certainly among the oldest and most enduring intergroup relations for both sides, the black–Jewish conflict is undeniably a complex, special case; but there are also black–Korean conflicts, black–Latina and –Latino tensions, and black–Chaldean rifts, of shorter duration, of course, though hurtful nonetheless.

The ready temptation is for commentators and critics to chide black folk for being ethnosaurs, upholders of ancient forms of racial complaint against every other group that has come to America and made it over us. The real story, of course, is that as black folk we *have* been stepped on and passed over. As Toni Morrison has eloquently reminded us, it is on the "backs of blacks" that America has been fashioned in such splendid economic privilege and cultural glory. So when I say black folk should turn the corner on the easy route of blame-the-Jew or blame-the-Korean, I don't mean we shouldn't raise tough questions. We should simply move from finger-pointing to serious analysis in discovering the source of our suffering.

When Kahlid Abdul Muhammad, former spokesman for Louis Farrakhan, finds a Jew behind every problem that plagues black folk, he is engaging in a highly imitative move ripped off from the worst proponents of black conspiratorial thinking throughout our history. That his verbiage is vicious is obvious, though he still strikes a chord in desperate black people who want to find some concrete reason for their plight. Why? Because we haven't done our homework.

While Muhammad manipulates the understandable human emotion to name the demon that vexes us—and when you're in bad shape, any demon will do—we fall farther from the truth of our condition. Jews are not our problem. Koreans are not our problem. Latinos and Latinas are not our problem. And though we have legitimate gripes with each group (as they do with blacks), what conscientious blacks have in common with conscientious Jews, Koreans, and Latinos and Latinas is much more interesting to ponder and exploit.

Turning the Corner

By forging alliances between such groups, substantive issues get debated and dealt with in ways that don't make the destruction of our opponents the way we gain cachet in our communities. And real conflicts surface that have much more to do with how power is distributed, how wealth is circulated, how influence is shared than with how your last name ends. The case of blacks and Jews is instructive. Blacks question why powerful Jews have sided with conservative southern politicians in opposing the renewal of the Voting Rights Act and important redistricting measures that would bring enhanced political power to black citizens. And blacks ask Jews why there is no outcry against these conservative Jews, nor is there a demand for Jews to renounce the potentially racist policies of their brothers and sisters.

Thus Jews ask blacks why their constant love affair with conspiracy makes them vulnerable to claims by some black intellectuals and leaders—from Leonard Jeffries to Louis Farrakhan—that Jews are the major roadblocks to black progress. Jews ask blacks why any criticisms of affirmative action are viewed automatically as racist, why blacks emotionally chafe when any suggestion that alternative strategies for black improvement are proffered. And Jews and blacks ask each other about the hierarchy of pain that grants privilege for each group's collective suffering, viewed in the Holocaust-versus-slavery debate, which often turns ugly and irrational. The point here is that we turn the corner on the acrimonious assaults on each other, and turn to more serious conflicts whose resolution might relieve the need of glorified pettiness on both sides.

But turning the corner also means that black folk have to come to grips with how we do one another in. Not simply in the ghettos of urban America, where black-on-black crime is much lamented and commented on, even if in ridiculously racist and sexist manners. The black-on-black crime I'm speaking about happens at the highest levels of intellectual and organizational endeavor. The deep distrust we harbor for one another—we still think white folk have some magic that black folk don't possess, whether in medicine or in marketing—makes us liable to vicious forms of professional backbiting and jealousy. It's the same for preachers and professors, lawyers and doctors, and journalist and judges. We kill with the pen as swiftly as we do with the Uzi.

This impulse to hurt those with whom we disagree, and with whom we share the greatest resemblance, is an ancient passion, a form of intolerance that only intimate contact can ignite. It's what killed Malcolm, this inability to disagree close-up without destruction. And there is so much at stake in our fights—identity, loyalty, passion, and love, as well as hatred, dissemblance, treachery, and betrayal.

We can turn the corner on the impulse to destroy what's black only by affirming the best of what's black—by offering simple economic measures that circulate black dollars in black communities; by taking a chance on black brothers and sisters in a professional service blacks have need of; by black parents insisting on excellence from their children in their schoolwork and social life; by refusing, consciously, to destroy the reputation of a brother or sister by speaking false or irresponsible words; and by heeding edifying, enabling criticism. This sounds, of course, so naive as to be incredible; but the ministration of a daily political ethic of care for fractured black bodies and spirits, as well as the sort of profound structural analysis and radical democratic social activity that I have advocated, is like Poe's purloined letter, made invisible because it lies hidden in full sight.

Such a political ethic of care might have saved Malcolm's life, might have enabled his promethean will to self-improvement and re-creation to be extended vastly into our bewildering wastelands of lost hope and surrendered faith. He was, after all, a holy man, a troublesome formulation to declare because religion—and rightfully so in many cases—is viewed with increased suspicion in our nation. But his hardheaded insistence on enlivening a black public theodicy, on delineating the shape and limits of black angst and rage against racial and economic injustice, makes his vision just right for our times.

If we are to turn the corner in earnest, ordinary black folk and leaders—local and national alike—must stop bashing young black people. The perennial evocation of a golden age of black ethical achievement, when the fabric of our common moral and social life was magically knit together, is certainly produced out of the whole cloth of utopian reverie. At every stage of our sojourn on American soil, black folk have appealed to a time, largely mythical and unquestionably romantic, when we were better than we are in whatever age in which we happen to be struggling. This understandable strategy of moral regeneration by harkening to past ideals is sometimes helpful and, as we're now discovering, sometimes quite harmful.

The present generation of young blacks has been rebuked and reviled for its fateful loss of a moral compass that had been bequeathed from one black generation to the next since slavery. They have been called a "lost generation," and damned for their violent self-destruction. Their hip-hop music has been scorned and attacked in a manner virtually unprecedented in our nation's history, and their culture has been viewed as damaged and pathological.

In turning the corner on our views of young blacks, we must acknowledge the incredible assault on mind and body that they have endured in ways hard to imagine for most adults. Although they are the victims of violence more than any other population, they are blamed for its vicious expression. Although they are caught in cycles of poverty that begin before they are born, their indigence is laid at the feet of their stubborn refusal to work. Although they are often born into families hardest hit by the postindustrial collapse and restructuring of industries that once provided stable work, their turn to informal economies to survive is viewed in coldly animalistic terms. And not just by white folk.

Most young black people want to do well, are afraid of a violent world, spurn self-destructive behavior, and aren't pathological. As we continue to demand the best of our young people, as we listen to them and *learn* from them, as we shed tears for them as they make mistakes while we recall our own foibles and failings, and as we continue to affirm their value as worthful human beings hampered from their best in a world determined, often, to snuff out their lives, we can help them survive to witness their children's prospering. Not without, however, a radical reorientation in our willingness to criticize capitalism and classism, and not without a willingness to sacrifice the comforts of our bourgeois, conservative black culture for a deeper analysis of why so few have so much while so many have so little.

Malcolm's greatest contribution to us is to think for ourselves, to learn to help ourselves when others refuse, and to demand a world in which such help is not the preserve of the privileged, but the domain of the masses. Malcolm's example still invites us to ask hard questions of ourselves, to renew ourselves at the altar of rigorous sacrifice and a shameless love of black folk. With the broad, humane vision that powered Malcolm's final days, African-American life can surge forward against the incredible odds we presently face. We can continue to reinvent ourselves as Malcolm reinvented himself. By our willingness to think and do the impossible in the name of the inextinguishable hope that moved our ancestors to dream and act with great boldness, we too can triumph, like Malcolm, by any means necessary.

Next booth =
t. Benn .
the case for
socialism . (see at
green Booth)
rub this out gently.

NOTES

Chapter 1

1. Bruce Perry, *Malcolm: The Life of a Man Who Changed Black America* (Barrytown, N.Y.: Station Hill Press, 1991).

2. Louis Lomax, *To Kill a Black Man* (Los Angeles: Holloway House, 1968); Perry, *Malcolm*.

3. Malcolm X, with the assistance of Alex Haley, *The Autobiography of Malcolm X* (New York: Grove Press, 1965).

Chapter 2

1. These personal and political understandings can be described as paradigms, or theories that explain evidence or account for behavior, that shift over space and time. For a discussion about paradigm shifts in the history of science, see Thomas Kuhn, *The Structure of Scientific Revolutions*, 2d ed. (Chicago: University of Chicago Press, 1970). According to Kuhn, revolutions in science occur when a given paradigm fails to account for an increasing degree of disconfirming evidence, called anomalies. Failure of the paradigm creates a crisis, and can be resolved only with the emergence of a new scientific paradigm. For an application of Kuhn's work to moral philosophy and religious experience, see Jon Gunnemann, *The Moral Meaning of Revolution* (New Haven: Yale University Press, 1979).

2. The lack of a significant body of scholarly literature about Malcolm reveals more about the priorities, interests, and limitations of contemporary scholarship than about his importance as a revolutionary social figure. There is no dearth of interest in Mal-

Notes

colm, however, in the popular press, and though cultural curiosity about him is now undoubtedly at a peak, he has unfailingly provoked popular reflection about his life and career among journalists, activists, and organic intellectuals since his death in 1965. This is made abundantly clear in two book-length bibliographies on Malcolm: Lenwood G. Davis, with the assistance of Marsha L. Moore, comps., *Malcolm X: A Selected Bibliography* (Westport, Conn.: Greenwood Press, 1984), and Timothy V. Johnson, comp., *Malcolm X: A Comprehensive Annotated Bibliography* (New York: Garland, 1986).

3. For an illuminating discussion of the philosophical issues and problems involved in understanding and explanation in the humanities, see Charles Taylor, "Interpretation and The Sciences of Man," in *Interpretive Social Science: A Reader*, ed. Paul Rabinow and William M. Sullivan (Berkely: University of California Press, 1979), pp. 25–71.

4. For the notion of thick description, see Clifford Geertz, "Thick Description: Toward an Interpretive Theory of Culture," in *The Interpretation of Cultures* (New York: Basic Books, 1973).

5. Michael Eric Dyson, "Probing a Divided Metaphor," in *Reflecting Black: African-American Cultural Criticism* (Minneapolis: University of Minnesota Press, 1993), pp. 115–128. For discussion of Malcolm's motivations for his autobiography, and Alex Haley's role in shaping the narrative of Malcolm's life, see also Arnold Rampersad, "The Color of His Eyes: Bruce Perry's *Malcolm* and Malcolm's Malcolm," and Robin D. G. Kelley, "The Riddle of the Zoot: Malcolm Little and Black Cultural Politics During World War II," both in *Malcolm X: In Our Own Image*, ed. Joe Wood (New York: St. Martin's Press, 1992), pp. 117–134, 155–175, respectively.

6. For more of my comment on other books about Malcolm, see Dyson, "Probing a Divided Metaphor," pp. 115–128.

7. For a good overview and discussion of these groups, see Raymond Hall, *Black Separatism in the United States* (Hanover, N.H.: University Press of New England, 1978).

8. For an excellent discussion of the links between Malcolm

Notes

X and the Black Power movement, of which he was a precursor, with discussions of SNCC, CORE, and the Black Panthers, see Robert Allen, *Black Awakening in Capitalist America: An Analytic History* (Garden City, N.Y.: Doubleday, 1969), pp. 21–88. For a discussion of the economic programs and comparisons of the social visions of each group, see Hall, *Black Separatism in the United States*, especially pp. 139–196.

9. See especially John Ansbro, *Martin Luther King, Jr.: The Making of a Mind* (Maryknoll, N.Y.: Orbis Books, 1982); Stephen B. Oates, *Let the Trumpet Sound: The Life of Martin Luther King, Jr.* (New York: Harper & Row, 1982); and David Garrow, *Bearing the Cross: Martin Luther King, Jr., and the Southern Christian Leadership Conference, 1955–1968* (New York: Morrow, 1986).

10. John Henrik Clarke, ed., *Malcolm X: The Man and His Times* (1969; Trenton, N.J.: Africa World Press, 1990).

11. Charles Wilson, "Leadership Triumph in Leadership Tragedy," in *Malcolm X*, ed. Clarke, pp. 36–37.

12. James Boggs, "The Influence of Malcolm X on the Political Consciousness of Black Americans," and Wyatt Tee Walker, "Nothing but a Man," in *Malcolm X*, ed. Clarke, pp. 52, 67.

13. Albert Cleage, "Myths About Malcolm X," in *Malcolm X*, ed. Clarke, p. 15.

14. Oba T'Shaka, *The Political Legacy of Malcolm X* (Richmond, Calif.: Pan Afrikan, 1983); Malcolm X, *The End of White World Supremacy: Four Speeches by Malcolm X*, ed. Benjamin Karim [Goodman] (New York: Arcade, 1971).

15. T'Shaka, *Political Legacy of Malcolm X*, pp. 244–245.

16. Ibid., pp. 57, 118.

17. Karim, Introduction to Malcolm X, *End of White World Supremacy*, pp. 21–22.

18. Gordon Parks, "Malcolm X: The Minutes of Our Last Meeting," in *Malcolm X*, ed. Clark, p. 120.

19. On his repudiation of the white devil theory, see Malcolm X, with the assistance of Alex Haley, *Autobiography of Malcolm X* (New York: Grove Press, 1965), pp. 362–363. For Malcolm's

desire to meet Robeson a month before his death, see Martin Duberman, *Paul Robeson* (New York: Knopf, 1988), p. 528.

20. I take up this issue in "Beyond Essentialism: Expanding African-American Cultural Criticism," in *Reflecting Black*, pp. xiii–xxxiii.

21. The debate about cultural and racial authenticity as it relates to who is able to interpret Malcolm's legacy legitimately has most recently occurred in writer-activist Amiri Baraka's attacks on Spike Lee about Lee's film portrait of Malcolm X before his film appeared. Implicit in Baraka's charges that Lee would not adequately or accurately represent Malcolm is the belief that Baraka's representation of Malcolm is superior. Baraka's hagiographical recollections of Malcolm and his refusal to concede that Lee's claims and representations of him may be equally valid are a prime example of the often insular intellectual climate surrounding debates about Malcolm. The irony here, of course, is that of all current black directors, with the possible exception of John Singleton, Spike Lee appears most suitably disposed to represent a vision of Malcolm that jibes with Baraka's cultural views, given Lee's Afrocentric film and aesthetic vocabulary and his neonationalist cultural perspective.

22. Malcolm X, "Answers to Questions at the Militant Labor Forum," in *By Any Means Necessary: Speeches, Interviews, and a Letter, by Malcolm X*, ed. George Breitman (New York: Pathfinder Press, 1970), pp. 22–23.

23. See Henry Young's two-volume study, *Major Black Religious Leaders* (Nashville: Abingdon Press, 1977, 1979).

24. Louis E. Lomax, *When the Word Is Given: A Report on Elijah Muhammad, Malcolm X, and the Black Muslim World* (Cleveland: World, 1963), and *To Kill a Black Man* (Los Angeles: Holloway House, 1968); James H. Cone, *Martin and Malcolm and America: A Dream or a Nightmare?* (Maryknoll, N.Y.: Orbis Books, 1991); Peter Goldman, *The Death and Life of Malcolm X*, 2d ed. (1973; Urbana: University of Illinois Press, 1979). For a discussion of moral saints, see Susan Wolf, "Moral Saints," *Journal of Philosophy* 8 (1982): 419–439, and Robert Merrihew Adam's response to her essay in

The Virtue of Faith and Other Essays in Philosophical Theology (New York: Oxford University Press, 1987), pp. 164–173.

25. Of course, the classic treatment of the Black Muslims during the leadership of Elijah Muhammad and Malcolm X is C. Eric Lincoln, *The Black Muslims in America* (Boston: Beacon Press, 1961, 1973). Also very helpful is E. U. Essien-Udom, *Black Nationalism: A Search for an Identity in America* (Chicago: University of Chicago Press, 1962). For a treatment of the Nation of Islam under Elijah Muhammad and Malcolm X, and it transition to orthodox Islamic practice and belief under Wallace Muhammad as the World Community of al-Islam in the West, see Clifton E. Marsh, *From Black Muslims to Muslims: The Transition from Separatism to Islam, 1930–1980* (Metuchen, N.J.: Scarecrow Press, 1984). For a historical and analytic treatment of the Nation of Islam, including its history under Muhammad and Wallace Muhammad, and its separate revitalization as the second incarnation of the Nation of Islam under Louis Farrakhan, see Martha F. Lee, *The Nation of Islam: An American Millenarian Movement* (Lewiston, N.Y.: Edwin Mellen Press, 1988).

26. Lomax, *When the Word Is Given*, pp. 87, 68.

27. For an extended review of Cone's book, see my essay "Martin and Malcolm," in *Reflecting Black*, pp. 250–263.

28. Of course, Malcolm's life and thought represented and addressed various aspects of both religious and revolutionary nationalism. In this regard, see John H. Bracey, Jr., August Meier, and Elliott Rudwick, eds., *Black Nationalism in America* (Indianapolis: Bobbs-Merrill, 1970), p. 505. Also see Essien-Udom, *Black Nationalism*. For a fine historical treatment of the heyday of black nationalism, see Wilson Jeremiah Moses, *The Golden Age of Black Nationalism, 1850–1925* (Hamden, Conn.: Archon Books, 1978).

29. Cone, *Martin and Malcolm and America*, p. 151.

30. Ibid., p. 170.

31. Other works explore the relationship between King and Malcolm, along with comparative analyses of other intellectual and religious figures, in a religious and social ethical context. For

two fine examples, see Peter Paris, *Black Leaders in Conflict*, 2d ed. (Louisville: Westminster Press/John Knox Press, 1991), and Robert M. Franklin, *Liberating Visions: Human Fulfillment and Social Justice in African-American Thought* (Minneapolis: Augsburg, 1990).

32. Ralph Ellison, quoted in Robert B. Stepto and Michael S. Harper, "Study and Experience: An Interview with Ralph Ellison," in *Chant of Saints: A Gathering of Afro-American Literature, Art, and Scholarship*, ed. Stepto and Harper (Urbana: University of Illinois Press, 1979), p. 458.

33. For insightful treatments of Du Bois, see Arnold Rampersad, *The Art and Imagination of W. E. B. Du Bois* (Cambridge, Mass.: Harvard University Press, 1976); Gerald Horne, *Black and Red: W. E. B. Du Bois and the Afro-American Response to the Cold War, 1944–1963* (Albany: State University of New York Press, 1986); Manning Marable, *W. E. B. Du Bois: Black Radical Democrat* (Boston: Twayne, 1986); and, of course, the definitive treatment of Du Bois to date, David Levering Lewis, *W. E. B. Du Bois: Biography of a Race, 1868–1919* (New York: Holt, 1993). For the definitive treatment of Booker T. Washington, see Louis Harlan's two volumes: *Booker T. Washington: The Making of a Black Leader, 1856–1901* (New York: Oxford University Press, 1972), and *Booker T. Washington: The Wizard of Tuskegee, 1901–1915* (New York: Oxford University Press, 1983).

34. Lomax, *To Kill a Black Man*, p. 10.

35. George Breitman, "More Than One Way 'To Kill a Black Man,'" in *The Assassination of Malcolm X*, ed. George Breitman, Herman Porter, and Baxter Smith (New York: Pathfinder Press, 1976), pp. 131–144.

36. Robert Franklin also makes use of Goldman's notion of public moralist in his excellent book *Liberating Visions*, a comparative study of Booker T. Washington, W. E. B. Du Bois, Malcolm X, and Martin Luther King, Jr.

37. There is a swelling literature on the possible plots and theories of how Malcolm was murdered. While the close study of this literature is beyond my purposes here, it certainly constitutes an intriguing category of debate around Malcolm. See, for ex-

ample, Breitman, Porter, and Smith, eds., *Assassination of Malcolm X*, and Karl Evanzz, *The Judas Factor: The Plot to Kill Malcolm X* (New York: Thunder Mouth Press, 1992).

38. For arguments that Goldman's views about Malcolm's assassination support the official government story, and that the CIA and the Bureau of Special Services (BOSS)—the name of the New York secret police agency at the time of Malcolm's death—were implicated in his assassination, see George Breitman, "A Liberal Supports the Government Version," in *Assassination of Malcolm X*, ed. Breitman, Porter, and Smith, pp. 145–166.

39. Goldman, *Death and Life of Malcolm X*, p. 191.

40. Martin Luther King, Jr., quoted in David Halberstam, "When 'Civil Rights' and 'Peace' Join Forces," in *Martin Luther King, Jr: A Profile*, ed. C. Eric Lincoln, rev. ed. (New York: Hill & Wang, 1984), p. 202.

41. Clayborne Carson, "Malcolm and the American State," in *Malcolm X: The FBI File*, ed. David Gallen (New York: Carroll & Graf, 1991), p. 18.

42. Ibid.

43. See George Devereux, *Basic Problems of Ethnopsychiatry*, trans. Basia Miller Gulati and George Devereux (Chicago: University of Chicago Press, 1980); Frantz Fanon, *The Wretched of the Earth* (New York: Grove Press, 1966), and *Black Skin, White Masks* (New York: Grove Press, 1967); Erich Fromm, *Beyond the Chains of Illusion: My Encounter with Marx and Freud* (New York: Simon and Schuster, 1962); Christopher Lasch, *The Culture of Narcissism* (New York: Warner Books, 1979); Bruce Brown, *Marx, Freud, and the Critique of Everyday Life: Toward a Permanent Cultural Revolution* (New York: Monthly Review Press, 1973); Margaret MacDonald, ed., *Philosophy and Analysis* (Oxford: Blackwell, 1954); and relevant work of the Frankfurt school, including Theodor W. Adorno, Walter Benjamin, Erich Fromm, Max Horkheimer, Herbert Marcuse, and Jürgen Habermas. For a collection of essays by these authors, see Andrew Arato and Eike Gebhardt, eds., *The Essential Frankfurt School Reader* (New York: Continuum, 1982). For a treatment of their work in relation to psychoanalytic theory, see C.

Notes

Fred Alford, *Narcissism: Socrates, the Frankfurt School, and Psycho-analytic Theory* (New Haven: Yale University Press, 1988).

44. Richard Lichtman, *The Production of Desire: The Integration of Psychoanalysis into Marxist Theory* (New York: Free Press, 1982), p. ix.

45. Ibid., pp. ix–x.

46. Erik H. Erikson, *Gandhi's Truth: On the Origins of Militant Nonviolence* (New York: Norton, 1969). For a more controversial psychobiographical treatment of a historical figure, see Erikson's study of Protestant reformer Martin Luther, *Young Man Luther* (New York: Norton, 1958).

47. Eugene Victor Wolfenstein, *The Victims of Democracy: Malcolm X and the Black Revolution* (1981; London: Free Association Books, 1989).

48. Ibid., pp. 1–2.

49. Ibid., p. xiii.

50. For an important historical examination of white working-class racism, see David R. Roediger, *The Wages of Whiteness: Race and the Making of the American Working Class* (London: Verso, 1991).

51. Other Marxist, socialist, and progressive approaches to race theory and racism attempt to theorize race as a socially, culturally, historically, and politically constructed category that undergoes change over space and time. See, for example, Cornel West, "Marxist Theory and the Specificity of Afro-American Oppression," in *Marxism and the Interpretation of Culture*, ed. Cary Nelson and Lawrence Grossberg (Urbana: University of Illinois Press, 1988), pp. 17–33; Lucius Outlaw, "Toward a Critical Theory of 'Race,' " in *Anatomy of Racism*, ed. David Goldberg (Minneapolis: University of Minnesota Press, 1990), pp. 58–82; Michael Eric Dyson, "The Liberal Theory of Race," and "Racism and Race Theory in the Nineties," in *Reflecting Black*, pp. 132–156; Leonard Harris, "Historical Subjects and Interests: Race, Class, and Conflict," and Lucius Outlaw, "On Race and Class, or, On the Prospects of 'Rainbow Socialism,' " both in *The Year Left 2: An American Socialist Yearbook*, ed. Mike Davis et al. (London: Verso, 1987); and Michael

Notes

Omi and Howard Winant, *Racial Formation in the United States: From the 1960s to the 1980s* (London: Routledge & Kegan Paul, 1986).

52. See Thomas Gossett, *Race: The History of An Idea in America* (Dallas: Southern Methodist University Press, 1965).

53. Wolfenstein, *Victims of Democracy*, p. 37.

54. Bruce Perry, *Malcolm: The Life of a Man Who Changed Black America* (Barrytown, N.Y.: Station Hill Press, 1991).

55. Ibid., p. ix.

56. Ibid., p. x.

57. Ibid., pp. 41–42.

58. Ibid., p. 54.

59. For further discussion of this subject, see Dyson, "Beyond Essentialism," pp. xiii–xxxiii.

60. For insightful discussions of the predicament of black intellectuals, see, of course, Harold Cruse's pioneering *The Crisis of the Negro Intellectual* (New York: Morrow, 1967); Cornel West, "The Dilemma of the Black Intellectual," *Cultural Critique*, no. 1 (Fall 1985): 109–124; and Jerry Watts, "Dilemmas of Black Intellectuals," *Dissent*, Fall 1989, pp. 501–507.

61. Christian ethicist Katie Cannon writes about the "white academic community's flourishing publishing monopoly on the writing of black history, black thought, and black world view. Black scholars did not abdicate their roles in these fields to white academicians. Blacks have written monographs, theses, conference papers, proposals, and outlines for books on various aspects of black reality since the 1700s, but white publishers did not give them serious consideration until the 1970s" ("Racism and Economics: The Perspective of Oliver C. Cox," in *The Public Vocation of Christian Ethics*, ed. Beverly W. Harrison, Robert L. Stivers, and Ronald H. Stone [New York: Pilgrim Press, 1986], p. 121).

62. William James, *The Varieties of Religious Experience* (1902; New York: Penguin, 1982).

63. Lomax, *To Kill a Black Man*, p. 142.

64. Goldman, *Death and Life of Malcolm X*, p. 189.

65. George Breitman, *The Last Year of Malcolm X: The Evolution of a Revolutionary* (New York: Pathfinder Press, 1967); Malcolm X,

Notes

Malcolm X Speaks: Selected Speeches and Statements, ed. George Breitman (New York: Pathfinder Press, 1965); *By Any Means Necessary;* and *Malcolm X: The Last Speeches*, ed. Bruce Perry (New York: Pathfinder Press, 1989).

66. Breitman, *Last Year of Malcolm X*, p. 69.

67. Malcolm, X, *By Any Means Necessary*, p. 159.

68. Breitman, *Last Year of Malcolm X*, p. 65.

69. Malcolm X, *By Any Means Necessary*, p. 159.

70. Given the variety and complexity of black nationalist thought, Malcolm could have accommodated and advocated such changes had he had sufficient time to link his broadened sense of struggle to the subsequent social and political activity he inspired. It is important, however, not to overlook the tensions between groups like SNCC and Malcolm while he lived. As Lomax says: "... Malcolm was never able to effect an alliance with the young black militants who were then plotting the crisis that is now upon the republic. His trip to Selma was arranged by SNCC people but no alliance resulted. The Black Power people would later raise Malcolm to sainthood but they would not work with him, nor let him work with them, in life" (*To Kill a Black Man*, pp. 157–158).

71. Breitman, *Last Year of Malcolm X*, p. 27.

72. Ibid., p. 34.

73. Malcolm X, *Malcolm X Speaks*, p. 128, quoted in Breitman, *Last Year of Malcolm X*, p. 35.

74. Malcolm X, "The Harlem 'Hate-Gang' Scare," in *Malcolm X Speaks*, ed. Breitman, p. 65.

75. Ibid., p. 69.

76. Malcolm X, *By Any Means Necessary*, pp. 159–160.

77. See Leon Trotsky, *Leon Trotsky on Black Nationalism and Self-Determination* (New York: Pathfinder Press, 1978).

78. C. L. R. James, interview in *Visions of History*, ed. MARHO (New York: Pantheon, 1984), p. 270.

79. I do not mean to rule out other genres in which Malcolm's life and accomplishments may be examined. For an example of a science fiction approach to his life and thought, see Kent Smith, *Future X* (Los Angeles: Holloway House, 1989),

which appears to have been influenced as much by Schwarzen-
negger's *Terminator* films as by ideological currents in African-
American culture.

Chapter 3

1. For insightful treatments of black nationalism, see John
Bracey, Jr., August Meier, and Elliot Rudwick, eds., *Black Nation-
alism in America* (Indianapolis: Bobbs-Merrill, 1970); Wilson Jer-
emiah Moses, *The Golden Age of Black Nationalism: 1950–1925*
(Hamden, Conn.: Archon Books, 1978); and Alphonso Pinkney,
Red, Black, and Green: Black Nationalism in the United States (London:
Cambridge University Press, 1976).

2. For useful treatments of the various stages and varieties
of black nationalism, see Moses, *Golden Age of Black Nationalism;*
John Bracey, Jr., "Black Nationalism Since Garvey," in *Key Issues
in the Afro-American Experience,* ed. Nathan Huggins, Martin Kilson,
and Daniel M. Fox (New York: Harcourt Brace Jovanovich, 1971),
vol. 2, pp. 259–279; and Mary Frances Berry and John Blassingame, *Long Memory: The Black Experience in America* (New York:
Oxford University Press, 1982), pp. 388–423.

3. Clayborne Carson, *In Struggle: SNCC and the Black Awak-
ening in the 1960s* (Cambridge, Mass.: Harvard University Press,
1981); Raymond Hall, *Black Separatism in the United States* (Hanover,
N.H.: University Press of New England, 1978); Robert Allen, *Black
Awakening in Capitalist America: An Analytic History* (Garden City,
N.Y.,: Doubleday, 1969); James Cone, *Black Theology and Black
Power* (New York: Seabury Press, 1969); William Van Deburg, *New
Days in Babylon: The Black Power Movement and American Culture,
1965–1975* (Chicago: University of Chicago Press, 1992); Hugh
Pearson, *The Shadow of the Panther: Huey Newton and the Price of
Black Power in America* (Reading, Mass.: Addison-Wesley, 1994).

4. Cited in "Malcolm X," *Newsweek,* November 16, 1992,
p. 72.

5. See especially, Lawrence Levine, *Black Culture and Black*

Consciousness: Afro-American Folk Thought from Slavery to Freedom (New York: Oxford University Press, 1977).

6. I realize that there are divisions in hip-hop culture and music, including hard-core, pop, black nationalist, and gangsta' rap. I am referring primarily to the black nationalist expression phase of rap, though Malcolm's influence is by no means limited to this subgenre of hip-hop.

7. Quoted in "A Tribute to Malcolm X" [special issue], *Black Beat Magazine*, 1992, p. 15.

8. Ibid., p. 13.

9. Ibid., p. 48.

10. The phrase is from Derek Bell, *Faces at the Bottom of the Well: The Permanence of Racism* (New York: Basic Books, 1993).

11. I am not suggesting that King was, by himself, the civil rights movement or that his accomplishments exclusively define its scope of achievements. I am suggesting that he is the most powerful symbol of the movement, however, and as a result was often the most visible target of Malcolm's attacks on its strategies, goals, and methods.

12. Quoted in "Tribute to Malcolm X," p. 13.

13. Ibid., p. 12.

14. C. Eric Lincoln, quoted in "Malcolm X," pp. 71–72.

15. C. Eric Lincoln, *The Black Muslims in America* (Boston: Beacon Press, 1961, 1973). Max Weber defined "theodicy" as the perception of incongruity between destiny and merit. In strict theological terms, theodicy has to do with justifying the ways of God to human beings, especially as a response to the problem of evil. As I use the term here, I view theodicy as the attempt by Malcolm X and the Nation of Islam to explain the evil of white racism and the suffering of blacks, by reference to an elaborate demonology of whiteness and a justification of the Nation of Islam's superior moral position in relation to white people.

16. Malcolm X, quoted in "Tribute to Malcolm X," p. 50.

17. Ibid, p. 49.

18. For my take on Jeffries, see my essay "Leonard Jeffries and the Struggle for the Black Mind," in *Reflecting Black: African-*

American Cultural Criticism (Minneapolis: University of Minnesota Press, 1993), pp. 157–163.

19. Ibid., p. 157.

20. I realize that Afrocentrism is a complex intellectual movement composed of many strands. However, I have in mind here primarily the views of its founder, Molefi Asante. For a sampling of Asante's views, see his *Afrocentricity: The Theory of Social Change,* 2d ed.(Trenton, N.J.: Africa World Press, 1990).

21. Quoted in "Tribute to Malcolm X," p. 12.

22. C. Delores Tucker, Dionne Warwick, Congresswoman Maxine Waters, and I, along with music professors and critics, testified before the U.S. Senate on gangsta' rap in 1994. I am basing my comments about their positions on their written testimonies, in possession of the author, delivered that day.

23. "Malcolm X," p. 70.

24. Ossie Davis, eulogy of Malcolm X, in *Malcolm X: The Man and His Times,* ed. John Henrik Clarke (1969; Trenton, N.J.: Africa World Press, 1990), p. xii.

25. Patricia Hill Collins, "Learning to Think for Ourselves: Malcolm X's Black Nationalism Reconsidered," in *Malcolm X: In Our Own Image,* ed. Joe Wood (New York: St. Martin's Press, 1992), pp. 62, 78.

26. For more comment on this aspect of King's legacy, see my op-ed "King's Light, Malcolm's Shadow," *New York Times,* January 18, 1993, p. 19.

27. I hope to sketch out briefly in this chapter and in Chapter 6 what I mean by radical democracy. Suffice it say the term seeks to accent the emancipatory elements of political practice, signifying a broad emphasis on popular participation in the affairs of the citizenry. For me, radical democrats view issues of race, gender, sexuality, the environment, the workplace, and the like to be crucial spheres where the negotiation over identity, equality, and emancipation takes place. My radical democratic principles commit me to a relentless quest for the sort of political behavior, economic arrangements, and social conditions that promote a full, productive life for the common citizenry. For a powerful vision

of radical democracy, and a defense of this term to express and unite a wide range of progressive politics, see Stanley Aronowitz's "The Situation of the Left in the United States," *Socialist Review* 23, no. 3 (1994): 5–79. See also the lively exchange between Aronowitz and several capable interlocutors, including Amarpal Dhaliwal, Barbara Ehrenreich, Barbara Epstein, Richard Flacks, Michael Omi, Howard Winant, and Eli Zaretsky, on pp. 81–150.

28. By now, of course, "sex," "race," and "class" are viewed as hackneyed terms meant to invoke an automatic knowledge of the problems to which they refer. The strategy of some critics is to dismiss the seriousness of these issues because of a terminological or ideological impasse. This strategy, I believe, is disingenuous and fails to account for the bleak persistence of sexism, racism, and classism. Indeed, I would argue that it is not that we have tried to employ sophisticated notions of the relationship between these spheres of social identity and theory, and public struggle, and they have failed, but that they have never been really tried, actually implemented. The debate over multiculturalism and its opponents has encouraged reactionary elements to seize the upper hand in the battle to describe our contemporary social landscape. But often, these critics fail to highlight either their own direct complicity in racism, sexism, or classism, or their participation in traditions of thought that supply the (sometimes subtle) rationale for these problems' bleak persistence.

29. See Uwe Reinhart, "Cut Costs? Of Course," *New York Times*, June 12, 1994, sec. 4A, p. 8.

30. For instance, see Toni Morrison, ed., *Race-ing Justice, Engendering Power* (New York: Pantheon, 1992).

31. I take up this issue in "Beyond Essentialism: Expanding African-American Cultural Criticism," in *Reflecting Black*, pp. xiii–xxxiii.

32. This does not deny the importance of forms of social activity and group behavior manifest in cultural activity such as play that represents subtle political resistance. For a highly creative analysis and application of a broadened notion of politics, especially among working-class black folk, see Robin G. D. Kelley's

Notes

brilliant *Race Rebels: Culture, Politics, and the Black Working Class* (New York: Free Press, 1994).

Chapter 4

1. On black popular culture, see Gina Dent, ed., *Black Popular Culture* (Seattle: Bay Press, 1992). See also my section on black popular culture in *Reflecting Black: African-American Cultural Criticism* (Minneapolis: University of Minnesota Press, 1993), pp. 1–111; Manthia Diawara, ed., *Black Cinema: Aesthetics and Spectatorship* (New York: Routledge, 1992); Mark Reid, *Redefining Black Film* (Berkeley: University of California Press, 1993); Ed Guerrero, *Framing Blackness: The African American Image in Film* (Philadelphia: Temple University Press, 1993); and Thomas Cripps, *Making Movies Black: The Hollywood Movie from World War II to the Civil Rights Era* (New York: Oxford University Press, 1993).

2. For my take on black men, see ''The Plight of Black Men,'' in *Reflecting Black*, pp. 182–194. See also Jewelle Taylor Gibbs, ed., *Young, Black, and Male in America: An Endangered Species* (Dover, Mass.: Auburn House, 1988).

3. A slew of recent films, from *Above the Rim* to *Inkwell*, also treat aspects of black male life. My analysis here is not an exhaustive engagement with the genre of male-centered films. Rather, I am attempting to provide a reading of dominant interpretive strategies within selected black films that address black masculinity.

4. For a discussion that provides the context for debates about black males, and the role the black independent press has in both fostering the debate and influencing black film, see my essay ''Between Apocalypse and Redemption: John Singleton's 'Boyz N the Hood,' '' in *Reflecting Black*, pp. 90–110.

5. For more extensive commentary on the history of hiphop, and critical discussion of rap's moral and political vision, see my *Reflecting Black*, pp. 1–22, 167–179, 276–281.

Notes

6. Of the many raps that explore these themes, see rap group Naughty by Nature's song "Ghetto Bastard."

7. Terry Williams, *Cocaine Kids: The Inside Story of a Teenage Drug Gang* (Reading, Mass: Addison-Wesley, 1989); Mike Davis, *City of Quartz: Excavating the Future in Los Angeles* (London: Verso, 1990).

8. Léon Bing, *Do or Die* (New York: HarperCollins, 1991).

9. For the notion of fictive kin, see Carol Stack, *All Our Kin: Strategies for Survival in a Black Community* (New York: Harper & Row, 1974).

10. For more on Lee's move from stereotype to archetype, and its consequences for his artistic vision and his treatment of film character, see my essay "Spike Lee's Neonationalist Vision," in *Reflecting Black*, pp. 23–31.

Chapter 5

1. See David Bradley's discussion of this struggle, and his role as one of the many hired and fired writers of the screenplay of Malcolm's life, in "Malcolm's Mythmaking," *Transition* 56 (1992): 20–46.

2. Ibid.

3. For an exploration of some of the themes of Lee's earlier work, see my essay "Spike Lee's Neonationalist Vision," in *Reflecting Black, African-American Cultural Criticism* (Minneapolis: University of Minnesota Press, 1993), pp. 23–31.

4. Malcolm X, with the assistance of Alex Haley, *The Autobiography of Malcolm X* (New York: Grove Press, 1964).

5. Bruce Perry, *Malcolm: The Life of a Man Who Changed Black America* (Barrytown, N.Y.: Station Hill Press, 1991). Malcolm confesses to this act not in his autobiography, but in a speech delivered a week before his death. See Malcolm X, "There's a Worldwide Revolution Going On," in *Malcolm X: The Last Speeches*, ed. Bruce Perry (New York: Pathfinder Press, 1989), pp. 122–123.

Notes

Chapter 6

1. I use the term "collective memory" in the way it is employed in contemporary historical and sociological scholarship. Barry Schwartz says that collective memory is "a metaphor that formulates society's retention and loss of information about its past in the familiar terms of individual remembering and forgetting. Part of the collective memory is, in fact, defined by shared individual memories, but only a small fraction of society's past is experienced in this way. Every member of society, even the oldest, learns most of what he knows about the past through social institutions—through oral chronicles preserved by tradition, written chronicles stored in archives, and commemorative activities (making portraits, statues, and shrines, collecting relics, naming places, observing holidays and anniversaries) that enable institutions to distinguish significant events and people from the mundane, and so infuse the past with moral meaning" ("Iconography and Collective Memory: Lincoln's Image in the American Mind," *Sociological Quarterly* 32, no. 3 (1991): 302.

2. Mary Frances Berry and John Blassingame, *Long Memory: The Black Experience in America* (New York: Oxford University Press, 1982), p. x.

3. Ibid., especially chaps. 1, 5.

4. Eric Foner, *Reconstruction: America's Unfinished Revolution, 1863–1877* (New York: Harper & Row, 1988), pp. 78–123.

5. I am not suggesting that these are the only expressions of heroism in African-American culture, but these two elements of African-American life are certainly the central poles of African-American heroic achievement.

6. Michael Kammen, *Mystic Chords of Memory: The Transformation of Tradition in American Culture* (New York: Knopf, 1991), p. 13.

7. Ibid., p. 122.

8. Ibid.

9. Frederick Douglass, quoted in ibid., pp. 121–122.

10. Barry Schwartz, "Social Change and Collective Memory:

Notes

The Democratization of George Washington," *American Sociological Review* 56, no. 2 (1991): 221.

11. George Herbert Mead, "The Nature of the Past," in *Essays in Honor of John Dewey*, ed. John Coss (New York: Holt, 1929), pp. 235–242; Maurice Halbwachs, *The Collective Memory*, trans. J. Ditter, Jr., and Vida Yazdi Ditter (New York: Harper Colophon, 1980).

12. Halbwachs, *Collective Memory*, p. 222.

13. Emile Durkheim, *The Elementary Forms of the Religious Life* (1912; New York: Free Press, 1965), pp. 415, 420; Edward A. Shils, *Tradition* (Chicago: University of Chicago Press, 1981), pp. 31–32.

14. Schwartz, "Social Change and Collective Memory," p. 222.

15. I am working on an ambitious project to wedge beneath stereotypes and statistics to deliver a complex, sophisticated analysis and interpretation of black males in *Boys to Men: Black Males in America* (New York: Random House, forthcoming [1997]).

16. See, for instance, Robert Staples, "Black Male Genocide: A Final Solution to the Race Problem in America," *Black Scholar* 18, no. 3 (1987): 2–11; and Jewelle Taylor Gibbs, ed., *Young Black and Male in America: An Endangered Species* (Dover, Mass.: Auburn House, 1988).

17. Quoted in James Cone, *Martin and Malcolm and America: A Dream or a Nightmare* (Maryknoll, N.Y.: Orbis Books, 1991), p. 89.

18. William Julius Wilson, *The Truly Disadvantaged: The Inner City, the Underclass, and Public Policy* (Chicago: University of Chicago Press, 1987); Mike Davis, *Prisoners of the American Dream: Politics and Economy in the History of the U.S. Working Class* (London: Verso, 1986).

19. Quoted in Cone, *Martin and Malcolm and America*, p. 89.

20. Malcolm X, *Malcolm X Speaks: Selected Speeches and Statements*, ed. George Breitman (New York: Pathfinder Press, 1965), p. 169.

INDEX

Index

Index

Index

Index

Goldman, Peter, 38, 46–48, 59, 65, 69
Gooding, Cuba, Jr., 112
Goodman, Benjamin, 34
Gospel music, 122–123
Graffiti, 83
Grandmaster Melle Mel, 83
Greer, Sonny, 57
Guinier, Lani, 156
Gumbel, Bryant, 93
Guns, as metaphor, 84

Hadj. *See* Mecca
Haitians, and Clinton policy, 155–156
Halbwachs, Maurice, 149
Haley, Alex, 13, 23, 55, 134, 186n.5
Hall, Albert, 137
Hampton, Lionel, 57
Harlem, 5
"Harlem 'Hate-Gang' Scare, The"
    (Malcolm), 70
Harlem Nights (Murphy), 136
Harmony, racial, 44–45
Harris, Leslie, 126
Health care, universal, 103
Hero, Malcolm as, 24, 29–30, 79, 82,
    139, 145, 150, 172
Heroism, in African-American culture,
    147, 201n.5
Hero worship, 74, 126, 140
Hill, Anita, 104, 105, 113
Hip-hop culture, 74, 82–83, 158
    attacks on, 182
    beginnings of, 83–84
    and black films, 115
    black masculinity in, 96
    divisions in, 196n.6
    gender relations in, 104
    lexicon of, 121
    rage in, 87
History, African-American, 61, 75
    black, 62, 92, 193n.61
    conspiracy theory of, 170
    writing of, 193n.61

History of the Russian Revolution
    (Trotsky), 71
Hollywood, and film on Malcolm, 130
Holocaust-versus-slavery debate, 179
Homeboy-from-the-hood
    backgrounds, xix
Homicide, black-on-black, 166, 168.
    See also Violence
Homophobia, xxii, 14, 58
    of gangsta' rap, 95
    of rap culture, 163
Homosexuality, Malcolm's alleged, 58,
    143
Horton, Willie, 157
Households, single-parent, 95
Human rights, 103
Human rights advocate, Malcolm as,
    14–15
Hustling tactics, Malcolm's, xv, 5–6,
    133, 135, 136, 137

Ice Cube, 112, 115
Identity
    black female, 108
    erosion of communal, 80
    male, 58
    national, 121
Identity, racial
    narrow visions of, 104
    search for, 90–91
    social construction of, 105
Identity politics, x
"I Have a Dream" (King), 27
Imprisonment, of black men, 108
Inequality, religious resistance to, 37.
    See also Equality
Infant mortality, 108
Influence, sharing of, 179
Injustice
    economic, 181
    religious resistance to, 37
Integration, vs. separation, 44
Integrationism, 44

Index

Index

Index

Index

Index

Index

Index

Index

UNIVERSITY OF WOLVERHAMPTON
LIBRARY